Jasper's Magical Christmas

Jasper's Magical Christmas

Benjamin Wardak

ISBN: 978-0-9997319-2-5

www.cometstales.com

Printed in the United States of America

First Printing 2021
First Edition 2021

To children around the world -
No matter what you are given in life,
you can make something wonderful of it!

May our Jasper remind all of us
that no matter what hardships we face,
we should keep going and never give up.
There is hope to hold onto,
a bright light shining just around the corner,
and for someone else, that shining light
might be you.

Just as Jasper shared his friendship and warmth,
you can shine your light for someone
by helping in your community,
sharing what you have with those who have less
or through small acts of kindness.
Work hard to reach your potential in life,
and as you blossom,
reach out and help those who are struggling
to blossom along with you.

Chapter 1

Twinkling lights reflected off the snow as Jasper crunched down the sidewalk. Angels and snowmen and Santas smiled at him merrily from the storefront windows, and each chilly breath he took smelled like holly and snow-dusted evergreens. He felt a gingery warmth rise in his chest. "Not again," he said.

As much as Jasper wanted to love Christmas, he couldn't help but dread it a little.

Jasper lived at McCallister's, the ramshackle orphanage on the outskirts of town. As far back as his memories could reach, he had never received a Christmas gift, or a birthday gift, or even something so simple as a friendly, "Happy Birthday." It was unlucky, he had learned, to be born on Christmas. People tended to forget that it was your birthday amid all the star-shaped gingerbread cookies, red-cheeked Christmas carols, and steaming hot chocolate.

He shoved his cold fingers into his pockets as he headed home. "Not that there are many cookies or carols or chocolates here," he mumbled to himself as he stomped his boots outside the orphanage door. He felt the air around him warm up as he stepped inside, but not by much – cold wind rattled the walls, and he felt the breeze slipping in from the cracks in the windows. A couple of runny-nosed boys darted around Jasper as if he were nothing more than a support beam. A taller boy chased close behind them. "Get back here, Mackies!" he shouted, using the name that the orphans affectionately called each other and that the village children hurled as an insult. Behind him called the scolding voice of one of the wards.

"I guess I can see why it's easy to forget things around here," said Jasper, who was so used to being ignored that he'd developed a habit of talking to himself.

But since Jasper's birthday was on Christmas, it felt as if it got double forgotten. The only person who never seemed to forget it was Jasper, although sometimes he wished he could. "Just remember, you won't be disappointed if you never hope for anything," he told himself. And he kept telling himself this every day as he walked through the bare halls of the orphanage, every day up until Christmas. But even without Santas at the orphanage, without angels or lights or the smell of cider and cloves, forgetting both his birthday and Christmas on the same day was more than Jasper could do. So, when Christmas Day finally came, Jasper did what he did every year. He waited for the sun to set. And when it did, when all the other boys were called inside to get ready for dinner, Jasper hid in the shadows.

Jasper waited, shivering, behind the somber spruce trees. He watched the lit windows of the orphanage, always secretly hoping to hear someone shout, "Hey, where's Jasper?" But when they didn't, and when the sky was dark and the clouds hid the stars and the snow glowed like silver in the faint light of the moon, he set out for his secret celebration.

Jasper carefully slipped through the rusted gate with its battered wooden sign that read: *McCallister's Orphanage*. Except the *-nage* at the end of *Orphanage* had faded long before Jasper could remember—and Jasper had lived there all eight years of his life—so it really read *McCallister's Orpha*, and that was all. Then, he headed down the long icy road heading into town, and running as fast as his feet could carry him. With every step, he could feel the loneliness of the orphanage pulling him back, but he refused to so much as glance over his shoulder. This was his birthday. This was Christmas. This was his one little gift to himself.

The icy road led Jasper between a scattering of houses, and he slowed to a walk. He drank in the sight of the merry light spilling out the windows to lay in golden squares on the snow. Like every year, there were strains of music drifting into the night, sometimes singing, sometimes a fiddle or a piano, and like every year, it was beautiful.

He passed the blacksmith's and the barber's, the baker's and the old carpenter's shop with wooden nutcrackers and Santas and angels crowding its windows. The little duck pond in the village center had frozen over six weeks ago, and village children had built half a dozen snowmen atop it. The snowmen stood still and frosty in the night. Jasper hurried past them toward the most splendid house in town: Mayor Shelby's house.

When he finally reached it, panting for breath, Jasper couldn't help the smile that burst across his face. It stood in front of the square, two stories tall, glittering with so many lights it took Jasper's breath away. "It's even more beautiful than last year," he whispered, his eyes dancing over the red, green, blue, yellow and white lights running along the eaves and down the doorposts, framing the windows and winding around the bare maple trees in the front yard. Wrapping his ragged scarf around his mouth, as if afraid that someone would spy his smile and snuff out his one little moment of happiness, he tip-toed past the maple trees. Through the front yard he went, up to one of the mansion's front windows, careful to duck in the shadows all the way even though the square was empty. Everyone else was home, celebrating.

Then, ever so slowly, Jasper peeked above the sill.

Inside the window was the most incredible sight of all. A Christmas tree stood beside the roaring fireplace, limbs hung heavy with ornaments. Beneath it were spread so many gifts that Jasper had to clap his hands over his mouth to smother his squeals of delight. Look how *many* there were! And all the different colors of wrapping paper! Even as he watched, one of the mayor's sons—George, the younger one—was tearing the silver paper off a gift. He threw the paper aside and held the gift up to the light: an airplane! It had the wonderfully shiny look of a toy shipped all the way from the big city, and its glossy paint shone handsomely in the flickering firelight.

Jasper jumped up and down, holding his hands over his mouth to keep any joyful cries from escaping. On the other side of the window, hugs were exchanged, the mayor's wife gave her son a kiss on the head, and George ran around the living room flying his plane through the air.

Bright-eyed, Jasper spread his hand in the air and moved it up and down, side to side, making a *whooshing* sound with his mouth. He spun in a circle with his eyes closed, imagining that he was holding a shiny new airplane with glossy paint. *It's for me,* he thought, his cracked lips breaking into a smile. *It's for me.*

Bess, the mayor's daughter who was around Jasper's age, unwrapped a gift next. Jasper's eyes followed every gleam of wrapping paper, hung on every smile. He was so absorbed in the moment that he forgot about the snow melting through his threadbare pants, the cold biting his hands through the holes in his mittens. Jasper glanced around to make sure no one was watching. He felt a little silly, but as Bess held up a velvety red dress, Jasper pretended that he, too, was holding up a new dress. Even if he didn't want to wear it, Jasper wouldn't have complained if someone gave him a dress, just so he could see how pretty the red velvet was, and how soft.

After Bess, Andrew, the elder of Mayor Shelby's sons, unwrapped a gleaming steel hatchet. Jasper's eyes lit up as bright as Andrew's. A hatchet! He had always dreamed of owning a hatchet. He imagined feeling the smooth handle and the weight swinging from the end of his arm as he carried it. He imagined the satisfying *thwack* it would make it as he swung it at a log to split or a tree to notch. Tears filled his eyes as he imagined that Mr. Shelby had given the hatchet to *him*. Mr. Shelby saying, "Here you go, son, I bought this for you in Devon," and putting his hand on Jasper's shoulder.

Jasper's smile trembled at the thought. No one had ever called him *son* before, or put their hand on his shoulder in that way, the way a father did to a son.

And so it went, gift after gift after gift. They piled up around the living room, shiny new toys from the city, handmade ballet slippers with silk ribbons, spices from some faraway place Jasper had read about in one of his books, new dresses and stockings and smart tweed jackets.

Jasper knew it was a foolish thing to think about, but he couldn't help wondering what it would be like to have so many *things*. To live in a house all your own—a mansion!—to have five different jackets and five different sweaters and five different pairs of pants, and more toys than you could possibly play with in one day, and a Christmas tree with lights. *I'd be happy with just one gift,* Jasper thought.

Then, he snapped to attention as Mrs. Shelby shepherded her children to the dining room for Christmas dinner. Jasper slipped over to the next window in time to see the family crowding around the table as Mrs. Shelby brought a steaming ham from the oven, all decorated with rosemary and cinnamon and slices of orange.

Jasper's mouth watered. He pressed his scarf to his ears so he wouldn't hear his stomach grumbling. *Ham.* He had never tasted ham, except the dreadful canned stuff that was delivered to the orphanage once a month by a stout man in a big black automobile. A red-faced Mr. Shelby cut slices of ham while Mrs. Shelby whisked a parade of colorful dishes from the kitchen.

As Andrew raised a fork of mashed potatoes to his mouth, Jasper raised his own hand with an invisible fork. He opened his mouth and took the invisible mashed potatoes. He chewed slowly, savoring the phantom taste as he watched Andrew chew and swallow. Jasper's mouth watered as he imagined the textures of ham, the gravy and rolls, and buttered beans on his tongue. Even as he was missing his own, real dinner, even as his own stomach churned with emptiness, Jasper never felt more full.

The Christmas firelight painted his face as he watched the family eat their Christmas dinner. Snowflakes fell onto his tattered cap and melted through his thin coat until little drops of water ran down his shoulders, but he didn't dare move. This was his birthday, and Christmas, and it only came once a year.

Finally, after watching the mayor's family laugh through dessert, watching Mrs. Shelby scolding George gently as he fired rolls with his new slingshot, and listening as Bess sang a few lines of some Christmas song he had never heard before all the children were herded upstairs to bed, Jasper clutched his coat around himself, shivering, and turned away from the window. He trudged along the side of the house through knee-deep snow. Before leaving, though, there was one more piece of his tradition, his gift to himself. He paused beside his favorite window.

It wasn't the brightest window, but to Jasper, it was the most beautiful one every year. Gentle blue and white lights shed their soft radiance over a nativity scene. Tiny tears rolled down Jasper's cheeks as he looked down on the little sheep and their shepherds, the three wise men bearing their gifts, Mary and Joseph and baby Jesus. Over the nativity scene rose a beautiful crystal angel.

Jasper put his hand to the glass. Gazing down at the crystal angel, he whispered the wish he made every year, the one he never gave up hoping for even though it had never come true, even in his dreams.

"I wish to see my parents. I wish to tell them I love them."

Jasper's numb lips trembled, and the tears rolled faster down his face. Jasper's hand fell away from the glass. He wiped his tears and wound his scarf around his face. He turned to make the lonely walk back to the orphanage, where he would have to sneak carefully up to his bedroom. His birthday Christmas tradition was over.

But behind Jasper, in the nativity scene in the window, something unusual happened. Although Jasper didn't see it, the angel began to glow. Her crystal wings gave the tiniest flutter, and a small sigh slipped out of her smiling lips. Then, she went still.

Chapter 2

"**G**oodbye, Jasper!" chirped a kindergartener named Peter. "Goodbye, Flynn! Goodbye, Bruce!"

"Where are you going?" asked Jasper. But then he saw a couple standing in the doorway, a wrapped box in their hands, grinning. "Oh," Jasper said.

Peter skipped toward them. "Don't forget your suitcase," the woman said, looking pleased with herself for sounding so motherly.

Jasper picked up the suitcase in the hallway and handed it to Peter. "Good luck, Pete," he said. He had only spoken to the boy two or three times – Peter had only been at McCallister's for a year. The young ones didn't stay long.

He watched out the window as orange leaves swirled from under the car as it rolled down the drive. Already, fall was coming to an end. Jasper had made it nearly through his eighth year without any families so much as giving him a second look. He knew that each year he grew older, the less likely he would be to ever find a family who wanted to adopt him. It was becoming more and more likely that he be a Mackie until, like the other older boys in the orphanage, he would look for work in town, or maybe move to the city and make his own living working in the steelworks or textile factories. But Jasper wasn't sure that those families who came into McCallister's were what he really wanted anyway. At least that was what he told himself. Sure, he wouldn't have minded a welcome home gift, or Christmas and birthday gifts, or even just one slice of Christmas pudding. But what Jasper really wanted was his real family. He knew that was impossible, though.

Soon, winter began creeping into the last autumn days. The days were growing shorter, and it was getting harder for Jasper to pull himself out of bed in the dark morning chill. That, and he could feel that dread setting in again. Christmas lights were going up around the village.

"A surprise is coming from Devon tomorrow," Headmistress Cicely announced one morning. She was a broad-shouldered woman with a thick bun of hair and, Jasper couldn't help noticing, fuzzy hair on her upper lip. He always thought that beneath her stern presence, there was a secret warmth to her. "If you all study quietly for the rest of today, you may have the day off when the surprise comes tomorrow."

A cheer went up among the children. They had been antsy recently as they felt the winter holiday approaching, hardly able to focus on their studies. That afternoon, though, excited as they were, they kept their heads down and their pencils moving.

What sort of surprise is it? Jasper wondered. He dared to hope. *Could it be a Christmas gift?* He waited impatiently, but quietly. You didn't get many surprises living at McCallister's Orphanage.

The next morning, Jasper got up as soon as night turned to gray dawn. He was going to be the first one to know what the surprise was. He hurried downstairs to find the headmistress already in her office.

"Good morning, Jasper," she said above her iron-rimmed spectacles.

"Good morning, Headmistress. Has the surprise arrived yet?"

The headmistress continued scribbling on the paper in front of her. "Not yet. It will be delivered mid-morning."

Jasper sighed. It would be *forever* until mid-morning.

"I have a small chore you can do to make the time pass faster," Headmistress Cicely said, as if she could read Jasper's thoughts.

Jasper liked it when the headmistress gave him chores. It meant that she thought he was responsible, which he tried very hard to be. And responsible? Well, he knew that also meant adoptable. "What chore?"

Headmistress Cicely held out a slip of paper. "Run this to the baker, and bring back the order of hot rolls he gives you."

"Are they cinnamon rolls?" Jasper took the slip of paper and looked at it. It was a check.

"No, not cinnamon rolls."

Jasper slid the check carefully into his pocket. He would have buttoned it closed, but the button had torn off last year. "I'll keep it safe, I promise. You can trust me."

The headmistress gave a thin smile. "I know, Jasper. Go on now. Take the cap that's on the door, it's brisk out there."

Jasper stood on his tip-toes to reach the cap on the door hook. He pulled it down over his ears. It was soft and warm. Maybe not so soft and warm as some of the caps the villagers wore, but much softer and warmer than his own. Another perk of running errands for the headmistress.

Jasper left the orphanage through the squeaky front gate and took the snowy road into town. In the square, he paused to watch men unloading crates and luggage from a wagon.

"Who's that?" Jasper asked Mr. Brewer, who, despite his name, made candles instead of ale.

"New folks in town," the stooped candlemaker said, squinting at the wagon. "Friends o' Mayor Shelby."

Mr. Brewer continued on his way, and Jasper stood a moment longer, watching the wagons being unloaded. The men were carrying the luggage into Mayor Shelby's mansion.

"Mr. Shelby's old friend Charles Gersham and his family," Mr. Willoughby the baker said as Jasper handed him the check.

Jasper always loved the smell of the baker's shop. Fresh dough and hot bread straight from the oven. "They're taking their luggage into the Shelbys' house," Jasper said.

Mr. Willoughby counted under his breath as he dropped rolls into a parchment sack. "The Gershams will be staying with the mayor's family until they finalize the payment on the house next door."

"They're moving here *permanently?*"

The baker shrugged. "Far as I've heard."

"But Widow Thorne lives in the house next door."

"She's moving to Devon, they say."

Jasper watched as the baker counted off the final roll and tied up the sack. "Don't you think she's too old to move to Devon?"

The baker laughed. He handed the sack across to Jasper. "Widow Thorne doesn't think so."

"Widow Thorne doesn't think she's too old to do anything," Jasper said. They shared a smile remembering the year before when she'd claimed she wasn't too old to ice skate.

"She was almost right!" laughed Mr. Willouhby. "She made it halfway across the pond on her feet before the skidded out from under her. You remember how she had to scoot the rest of the way across on her rump?"

Jasper giggled. The baker took an extra roll from his rack and tossed it to Jasper. "Payment for letting Headmistress Cicely keep her feet dry."

"Thanks," Jasper said. He turned at the door. "There's room for all the Gershams in the Shelbys' house?"

"Seems a decent big house, don't you think?" the baker said.

Jasper looked through the door glass at the mansion across the square. The Shelbys had spare rooms to put up their friends, but not even a slice of Christmas ham for the orphans at McCallister's?

"Besides," the baker said, "the Gershams only have one son."

Jasper bid the baker farewell and stepped out onto the sidewalk, directly into the path of some running boys. One of them knocked into him, and Jasper staggered against the wall of the baker's shop. His old shoes lost grip on the icy walk, and next thing he knew, he was sitting on his bum in the snow.

"Watch where you're going, rag bucket!" one of the boys called.

"Hey look, it's Jasper!"

Jasper scrambled to his feet and gathered the parchment sack of rolls. Eyes down, he tried to shuffle away, but one of the boys slapped his arm.

"Look at me when I'm talking to you," a tubby boy with

curly black hair said. His name was Sebastian. He was a farmer's son. When Jasper was five, Sebastian had run over Jasper's pet frog with his bicycle. Sebastian didn't remember it, but Jasper did.

Jasper looked into Sebastian's eyes and said nothing.

"Come on, Sebastian," another boy called. It was Andrew, Mayor Shelby's older son.

"Grubby Jasper just ran into Henry and didn't apologize," Sebastian said imperiously. He always called Jasper 'Grubby Jasper', as if it were clever.

Jasper glanced around at the other boys. There were five of them, all common faces around the village except for one tall, red-haired boy who Jasper assumed to be Henry. "Sorry," he muttered, "it was an accident."

The red-haired boy pushed Sebastian playfully away from Jasper. "Lay off, Sebas, he's fine." He plucked the roll from Jasper's hand, the one the baker had given him as a gift. "I'll take this as payment," he said with a grin. He tore off a bite of steaming roll.

Andrew called again and the boys went on their way, jostling and laughing.

Jasper straightened his coat and hurried back to the orphanage, his hands clutched around the parchment sack, his stomach grumbling. Before he even arrived at the gate, he could hear the clamoring of the other children outside. Then he saw it. There was a green delivery truck pulled up in the orphanage's driveway.

Chapter 3

J asper rushed to join the flock of children. The surprise had come, and he didn't want to miss it. Two delivery men were relaying crates to the orphanage matrons as the children followed, jumping and shouting.

"Ice skates!" someone cried. "Ice skates for all of us!"

Jasper's heart jumped in his chest. He craned his neck to see over the heads of the taller kids as the matrons opened the crates on the front steps. Most of the crates had already been opened, and the lovely white of brand new skates flashed everywhere as children fought over who got what pair. Headmistress Cicely was waving her arms and calling for order, trying to say something about taking turns, but that was the thing about surprises: they created excitement, and excitement at McCallister's Orphanage usually meant chaos.

Jasper shoved the sack of rolls into the headmistress' hand. "Here you go!" he shouted, and he dove into the melee. He found a pair of unclaimed skates and escaped to the side of the orphanage with them, where he sat in the snow and strapped them around his feet. He couldn't stop grinning. How long had it been since he'd been able to ice skate? He remembered ice skating once years ago, when Mayor Shelby's wife donated her children's old skates to the orphanage. All fifty-four orphans had taken turns on those three pairs of skates.

This time, they all had their *own*. Around the corner, Jasper could hear Headmistress Cicely saying something about being grateful to someone named Ms. Preston, who seemed to be a skate maker in Devon. There was something else about a charity, but Jasper could hardly hear over his own excitement. He tightened the final knot and stood up, laughing at the wonderful wobbly feeling of standing on snow in ice skates. They were a little snug, but he didn't care. Grinning, he hobbled back around to the front of the orphanage.

It was a mess. Empty crates, crate lids, and sawdust were scattered everywhere. The delivery truck had driven off sometime amid the commotion. Children sat everywhere—on the steps, in the doorways, on the snow—trying on their skates. Matron Simmons was bustling around calling, "No need to push, there's enough for everyone! Be patient, you'll get yours!"

Those with their skates already on were calling to Headmistress Cicely, "Can we go to the pond? Can we go to the pond?" And she was shouting something back, but Jasper couldn't hear over the commotion.

And then, abruptly, all the crates were empty, and the last of the ice skates was being laced up. Jasper noticed a little boy standing on the top step, his eyes wide, his hair sticking up as he gripped his hat nervously. "Headmistress?"

Headmistress Cicely looked up from where she sat helping a girl put on her skates. "Yes, Robin?"

The boy's lip trembled. "Where are mine?"

The Headmistress looked left and right at all the empty crates and scattered lids.

"We'll find them, Robin," motherly Matron Simmons said. She began bustling from crate to crate, searching through the sawdust. The other matrons joined her, and then the head-mistress too. But Jasper knew what had happened before they finished searching: there had been a miscount. There weren't enough skates. Robin must have known too, because he sat down on the front steps and began to sob.

Headmistress Cicely hurried over to him. "Hey now," she said, sitting beside him, "we'll take turns. You'll get to skate."

Jasper wondered how, after all these years running the orphanage, she still didn't understand. Sharing didn't fix anything. All Robin knew was that there weren't enough for him. He had been forgotten.

When you'd been forgotten all your life, even a small thing like ice skates could mean a lot one way or another.

Jasper bit his lip. He balanced on his silver blades, imagining that he was gliding across the ice of the pond. He closed his eyes for a moment and soaked in the feeling of having something new of his very own.

Then, Jasper sat down and undid the knots. "Here you go," he said, handing them to the small boy on the steps. "They're yours. Your very own."

Robin looked up at him with red eyes. "You don't have to share."

"I'm not sharing," Jasper said. That was important. "I'm giving them to you."

Robin's lip trembled. He wiped his eyes and his snotty nose. "Thank you," he sniffled, taking the skates slowly. He clutched the skates possessively against his chest.

An hour later, Jasper sat beside the big pond at the east end of the village. In spring it was full of ducks and trout, but it was the end of November now, and it had been frozen over for a month. Today, it was so crowded with skaters that Jasper was surprised there weren't more collisions.

He patted snow into a ball beside him, then broke it apart with his fist. He pulled his scarf up over his ears and wriggled his toes to make sure he could still feel them. He tried for the third time to count all the skaters on the pond but got lost around sixty. Fifty orphans plus at least three dozen village children, all red-cheeked and laughing as they swirled around.

Jasper found Robin amidst the smiling faces. The little boy whooped and giggled as he spun on the ice. Jasper smiled, and for a moment, he didn't feel so lonely. But only for a moment. His smile faded as he looked with glazed eyes at all the skaters. Had they all forgotten that he didn't have skates? Hadn't the other orphans seen him give his skates to Robin?

"I'd like to skate," Jasper mumbled to himself. "Even for a few minutes."

Ten more minutes passed, and it was as if the girls and boys he lived with every day had forgotten he existed. None of them offered their skates. None of them even looked his way.

There was one perk, at least, to being invisible, which was that no one noticed when you went missing. Jasper was just about to wander off to his secret hideout in the woods, when someone sat down beside him. He looked over in surprise. "Hi?"

The girl gave him a funny look. "Is that a question?"

Jasper stared owlishly. It was Bess, Mayor Shelby's daughter. The *mayor's* daughter. She was wearing a black pea coat buttoned over her powder blue dress and checkered stockings. Her cap was blue to match her dress, and her yellow curls puffed out around its fringe. "Hi," Jasper said again, trying not to sound so awkward this time. He felt glad that his cheeks were already pink with cold, or they would have surely turned red as he thought about the years of Christmases he'd spent peeking in through the Shelbys' window. He thought of Bess tearing the paper off each one of her gifts. Velvet dresses, silk bonnets, porcelain dolls, ballet slippers...

She's seen me! Jasper thought, suddenly. *She recognized me as that boy who comes and peeks in her window, I know it. She's here to scold me, and I'll never be able to go back.*

But instead, the girl offered her mittened hand. "I'm Bess," she said.

Jasper knew that, of course. He felt self-conscious of his own gloves, worn thin with his fingernails poking holes at the ends of his fingers, as he shook her hand. But he tried to act natural. "I'm Jasper," he said. "Why aren't you skating?"

"I hate skating," Bess said, puffing out her lip. "When I was five, I fell and broke my arm. We had to go into the city to get it set right. I'm always afraid I'll fall again. Besides." She picked up some snow and patted it into a ball. "It's much more fun to throw snowballs."

Bess winked at Jasper and hurled her snowball at her older brother as he skated by. Andrew dodged. He twisted and made a face at Bess, who stuck out her tongue at him. She aimed for her younger brother next, and George wasn't so quick as Andrew. The snowball hit him square in the shoulder. Bess laughed. "Come on, Jasper!"

Jasper smiled uncertainly. He packed a snowball and waited until a boy he knew from the orphanage skated by, then threw it timidly. It splatted harmlessly onto the ice.

"Oh, come on," Bess said, scrambling to her feet so she could throw harder. "If I can hit them, so can you."

Jasper flushed and got to his feet too, pressing another snowball. He picked a boy out of the skaters and hurled his snowball. It broke against the boy's leg, and Bess laughed. "Yes!" she cried.

Grinning, Jasper hurried to make three more snowballs.

He hurled them one after the other. Two skidded off the ice, but the third hit a girl from the orphanage in the shoulder. She jerked in surprise, nearly lost her balance, then caught it at the last moment. A laugh bubbled up in Jasper's throat. He patted another snowball.

"At the same time!" Bess cried. "Him!"

They both threw their snowballs at a village boy in a blue coat. Both hit him, and he skated away crying playful revenge. Before long, Jasper was throwing snowballs as quick as Bess, laughing and crying congratulations whenever she hit someone.

"Andrew!" Bess shouted, red-cheeked and grinning.

Jasper threw his too early, but it forced Andrew to spin right into the path of Bess'. Snow shattered across his chest. Bess whooped and gave Jasper a high-five.

"Him!" Bess was already packing her next snowball, pointing at a tall boy wearing a green cap. The boy skated a wide circle, passing close to the edge of the pond where Jasper and Bess stood, oblivious. Jasper and Bess drew their arms back at the same time, but Bess threw first. Her snowball flew unnoticed behind the boy.

But Jasper's hit him square on the side of the head. The boy turned, laughing, thinking Bess had hit him. When he saw it had been Jasper, his smile fell into a scowl. "Was that *you,*

Mackie?" he demanded. He whipped off his cap and skated expertly over to the edge of the pond, the side of his face red from where Jasper's snowball had hit it. "Did *you* just throw a snowball at me, Grubby Jasper?"

Jasper's heart plummeted as he recognized the tall boy with red hair peeking out of his cap. His mind raced for a name. *Had the baker said it? No, Sebastian had. Henry. The boy's name is Henry.*

"Huh?" Henry said, staggering up onto the bank in his skates. He shoved Jasper in the chest. "How dare you throw snowballs at someone who's more important than you, little orphan boy?"

Jasper shrank back, but Bess stepped angrily in front of him. "Leave him alone, Henry! You've always been a big bully, you know that? Jasper's my friend, and he's not less important than you. You've just been more lucky is all." She held another snowball in her hand, and she smacked it straight into Henry's face. "Bug off."

Henry scrubbed the snow from his face, staring daggers at Bess. His jaw clenched, but he didn't say anything. He gave Jasper a glare, then spun and skated away.

"Sorry," Bess muttered as she packed another snowball. "Henry's father is friends with my father. His family is visiting right now."

Bess resumed throwing snowballs, but the playful spirit had gone out of Jasper. He sat in the snow, not knowing
how to feel. Bess had just called him her *friend*. He had never
been called *friend* before. He felt a warmth in the pit of his
stomach, the glowing feeling of being noticed and chosen by
someone. But as he watched Bess, her curls bouncing and her
cheeks dimpling with each snowball she threw, he grew uneasy.
Wouldn't a girl like her be embarrassed to be friends with a boy
like him? Would she have to stand up for him all the time? He
certainly didn't want her to be friends with him because she
felt *bad* for him. Was there anything he had to offer her?

"Want to go to the bonfire?" Bess asked suddenly.

"Me? What?" Jasper asked, shaking himself from his thoughts.

"Someone started a bonfire in the square," she said.
"Let's go see!"

Jasper stood and dusted himself off. He scanned the pond,
but the matrons were all busy helping younger Mackies that
were shivering in the cold or had lost their balance and slid
on their new skates. On such an eventful day, he was sure no
one would notice if he slipped away for a while. Still, he felt
the rush he felt when he snuck out to the woods or, well, on
Christmas night. *Will I ever be able to do that again?* Jasper
wondered all of a sudden. *Does being friends mean giving up my
gift to myself?*

But Jasper couldn't turn down friendship. "Sure," he said, and he followed Bess uncertainly, watching her checkered stockings and powder blue skirt swishing against the snow.

"What is it like at the orphanage anyway?"

The question startled Jasper. Usually people either called him names or they tiptoed around the truth of the matter as if they were trying to pretend he was not an orphan at all. But here was Bess, whose life Jasper had imagined himself in over and over, and she wanted to know about *his*.

"Um…nice," he said, then wondered why he had said it. It wasn't nice, not at all. It was cold and dim and creaky, but Jasper could stand that. What really wasn't nice, Jasper thought, was how terribly lonely he felt there.

A few people trickled into the town square and made their way toward the bonfire. Jasper wanted to stand near it and feel the warmth on his fingers and cheeks. But he hesitated and hung back in the shadows.

"Hm," Bess said, stopping alongside him. "What do you do for fun there?"

"I like to read," Jasper said. He didn't tell her that he hadn't had a new book to read in two years. He didn't want her to understand what it was really like at the orphanage. If she knew, maybe she would really understand how huge the huge chasm was that separated them.

"Really?" Bess was saying. "I'm quite fond of reading myself. Andrew says reading is boring, and George is just learning, so I suppose that makes me the bookworm of the family. I think books are just lovely."

Jasper grew more at ease, and they crept toward the fire and held their hands out. No one seemed to notice him there, either, and Jasper was glad. He had attention from someone, and it was good attention, and the someone was not just any someone. It was a someone who used words like *quite fond*, and *lovely*. Nobody at the orphanage used such nice words.

"Do you ever go into the woods?" Bess asked, lowering her voice a little, as if to stop anyone from overhearing them.

"I made a hideout in a bramble patch," Jasper said. "There's a little tunnel through the brambles to get to it. Once you come out of the tunnel, you're in the middle of the bramble patch, so no one can get to you. I piled up some branches and made a little fort . . . ." He trailed off, imagining how juvenile he sounded.

But Bess' eyes were glowing. "A fort? Really? Maybe we can—"

"Bess?" A woman's voice drifted across the square, interrupting her.

Jasper looked past the bonfire's leaping flames to see Catherine Shelby, Bess' mother, beckoning. She had a wooly shawl clutched around her shoulders.

Mrs. Shelby noticed Jasper standing beside Bess, and a look of distaste crossed her face, as if she'd just seen a dead rat, or maybe a live one.

"Time for supper, dear," she called. "Hurry on."

Bess waved to Jasper then darted away, gone as suddenly as she had come.

Chapter 4

At the orphanage that night, Jasper lay awake after all the other boys had fallen asleep, tired from their afternoon of skating. He stared at the crack in the ceiling, the one he always stared at when he couldn't sleep. The mood around the orphanage had been festive after returning from the pond. Everyone had been laughing and smiling, wiping the ice from their skates, talking about the twirls they'd been trying to master and everything else fun that Jasper hadn't been able to participate in. He felt on the outside of the happiness, as if it were a river's current sweeping past, and he couldn't jump in.

But he had another reason to be happy. *Bess called me her friend.* Jasper smiled in the darkness and pulled his threadbare blanket up to his chin. He was happier than he had been in a long time. Even happier than last Christmas when, after watching Mayor Shelby give Andrew a gleaming new hatchet, Jasper spent the next week pretending it was *his* hatchet, tromping through the woods and swinging its imaginary blade from side to side, hitting branches and…

That had been fun, yes, but after a week, Jasper had sighed and admitted the truth. The hatchet was Andrew's, not his, and all these days he'd been pretending to chop off branches with it, well, no branches were chopped off. Not really.

But this, now, this was real. Bess really *had* called him friend. It wasn't in his imagination. He should be happy, right? Jasper sighed. The problem was, he was good at imagining, but he wasn't so good at the real world. What were friends supposed to do, anyway?

Filled with anxious energy, Jasper rolled over on his creaky mattress. When he saw Bess next, should he wave and say hello? Or would that be too forward? Maybe he should let *her* be the one to say hello first.

"Would you quit rolling around?" Jasper's roommate, Edgar, grumbled through the darkness. "Go to sleep."

Jasper sighed and closed his eyes.

When the first rays of morning sunshine shone through the window, Jasper leapt out of bed. He pulled on his raggedy coat and rushed downstairs, careful to avoid the thirteenth stair, which was loose and might fall out if you stepped on it wrong. He rapped on Headmisstress Cicely's door.

"Yes?" she called in her reedy voice.

Jasper stuck his head in. "May I go into town, Headmistress?"

Headmistress Cicely peered at him over her iron-rimmed spectacles. "We have class today, Jasper."

"You... you don't have any errands for me to run?" Jasper asked. "It's just, well, the village children are already on holiday, and I thought maybe..."

"I'm sorry, Jasper, but you know we must finish our first semester readers before we go on holiday for Christmas," the headmistress said. "And there are the winter essays to finish as well, and the seasonal arithmetic exams—"

"I've finished my reader," Jasper said, then he clamped his mouth shut, afraid the headmistress would scold him for interrupting. But she didn't, so he went on. "I've read to the very last chapter, I promise." It was true. He had finished it months ago, when the other kids were still muddling around chapter three. "I can finish my essay this evening, and the arithmetic—"

"Jasper."

Jasper's hope wilted.

The headmistress gave him an understanding smile. "I know how you feel."

But she didn't, she really didn't. This was his one chance to have a friend, and he was going to lose it because of *arithmetic*? Bess wanted him to show her his hideout in the woods, she'd been about to say so when her mother called her in to supper. "Yes, Headmistress?" Jasper said faintly.

"I know you're a brilliant reader, I really do. But I can't let you go play in town while all the other students must stay here and study. You know that wouldn't be fair."

"But I'm *done* with my reader!"

"Imagine how the younger students or those who aren't as good at reading would feel if I started letting all my brightest students go play as soon as they finished? I'll tell you what. You can have a choice. You may attend class today as usual, or you may assist the other students with their studies."

"Yes, Headmistress." Jasper sighed and returned to his bed.

He sat staring forlornly out the window until the other boys woke up. He ate breakfast at a table all alone, wondering what Bess was doing. He imagined her eating steaming biscuits with butter and cinnamon. She'd have crispy ham or crackling bacon as well, no doubt. He imagined her heading out to the square to look for him. When she didn't find him there, she'd shrug and go to play with her other friends. Then, she'd forget all about him.

In arithmetic, Jasper asked Edgar if he wanted any help. "I don't need your help, Mack," Edgar snapped, even if it was clear that he did. The problem was that the boys here were often proud and stubborn. They had to be.

Jasper was on his way to the lower classroom to see if perhaps that boy Robin who'd accepted his ice skates or one of the other younger boys might need help, when he ran into Headmistress Cicely.

"Just who I was looking for," she snapped. Then, she handed him a parcel. "For the post office," she said. "Quickly, please."

Jasper literally ran all the way into town, the parcel in its brown paper and strings bouncing under his arm. He gave it to the postman behind the glass window, and the postman gave him a wink and a candy cane. Jasper smiled and started to unwrap it, but decided instead to slide the candy cane into his pocket. *For Bess.*

He stepped out of the post office and looked down the street. People went about their daily business, dressed in charming long coats and ruffs in so many lovely colors. They all had cozy mittens and fuzzy caps, checkered scarves and snug boots to keep their feet warm and dry. Jasper didn't see Bess, so he turned down the street and made his way toward the town square. There, a man sold candied apples, and smiling mothers sent their children with a few pence. Jasper sat on a step and watched as the children ran around laughing, sticky red syrup around their mouths, wondering what candied apple tasted like. He felt as if he'd had one, many years ago, but he had been too young to remember it properly.

Remembering that the headmistress expected him back, Jasper got up and crossed the snowy square to Mayor Shelby's mansion. He stood at the gate and stared up at the splendid house. Icicles hung from its eaves, and firelight glowed in its windows. He waited for a few minutes with the unrealistic hope that Bess would happen to walk by a window, look down, and see him waiting there, but he saw no sign of her.

Jasper was about to leave when he was jolted out of his reverie by a cuff on the ear. "Ow!"

He grabbed his ear, then turned to see the freckled face of Henry Gersham. "Keep your grubby hands off Bess," he said, giving Jasper another push in the chest.

Jasper's spirit wilted. He abandoned hope of seeing Bess in

exchange for hope of an easy getaway from Henry. But as he turned to walk away, Henry stayed by his side.

"Don't you know Bess' father is the mayor, clodhead? Mayors' daughters don't play with Mackies." Henry pushed Jasper's shoulder.

"Leave me alone," Jasper muttered, walking faster.

"Hey, I'm talking to you, orphan boy!" Henry's foot flicked out, and suddenly Jasper found his legs all tangled up. He tripped and splashed into a muddy wagon track. "Oops," Henry said. "Did you slip, Mack? No matter. It's not like you can get any dirtier."

Jasper picked himself up and started running. His heart whirred with the terrible thought that Henry was chasing him. But when he glanced over his shoulder, he saw that the Gersham boy had turned back toward Mayor Shelby's mansion. Henry swung open the gate and ambled through that charming front yard with its neatly trimmed shrubs, soon to be strung with Christmas lights. Tears blurred Jasper's vision. *Don't watch*, he told himself, and he made himself run faster. He hated the thought of Henry going up those curving front steps and knocking on the Shelbys' door. He imagined Bess coming to open it and Henry smiling at her.

It wasn't *fair*. Jasper had done nothing wrong, nothing to deserve the orphanage. Henry had done nothing right, nothing to deserve a room in the Shelbys' mansion or supper at Bess' table. There was no reason to it, but there was also nothing Jasper could do to change it.

He ran all the way back to the orphanage with his muddy knees and muddy coat. Before going inside, he wiped the mud off in the snow outside as best as he could. He didn't want the headmistress or any of the matrons to notice and ask questions. Questions would only humiliate him, and even if he told the full truth, there would be no punishment for Henry Gersham. It was alright to punish dirty orphans, but if a boy's father had money, you didn't go scolding him. And Henry's father had money, Jasper was sure. Why would he be Mayor Shelby's friend if he didn't have money?

There were no more chances to see Bess that day, and when the next day came Jasper found himself watching snow swirl by the window while the other students struggled with their ABCs. He ran his fingernail along a groove in his wooden desk. The wood had begun to chip and peel years ago, and other boys had occupied themselves carving things into the desktop: their names or initials, hearts and stars, and one snowman that Jasper made a little deeper everyday by running his fingernail along its curving lines.

All that day, too, Jasper couldn't get the hope of having a friend out of his head. When he looked out the window and watched snowflakes danced against the glass, he wondered if Bess still remembered his hideout in the woods. When dark fell early and Jasper sat in bed reading a tattered book from the orphanage's pitiful library for the third time, he wondered if Bess sat reading in the mayor's stately library. And most of all, he worried that if he and Bess didn't have fun again soon, she would forget whatever it was that had made her call him a friend and remember that he was just a poor Mackie who wasn't supposed to talk to the mayor's daughter. It was almost enough to make him want Henry to call him names again, just for the chance that Bess would throw another snowball into Henry's face.

It wasn't until night, when Jasper closed the book and tucked it into the little nook beside his bed, that he stopped thinking about Bess. For every night before falling asleep, Jasper would close his eyes and try to remember his parents. Their voices, their faces, the feel of the skin on their palms, anything. Even if he couldn't remember them when he was awake, he thought, if he tried very hard, maybe he would remember them in his dreams.

Chapter 5

"Jasper?"

Jasper looked up from his essay. He had finished writing it half an hour ago and had been sitting quietly, listening to the other kids' pencils scribbling. "Yes, Headmistress?"

The headmistress leaned close to him so as to not disturb the kids still writing their essays. "Would you like to run an errand for me?"

Jasper flew out of his chair. "Yes, please!" He blushed when a few kids glanced at him in curiosity. He hadn't meant to say it so loud.

"I need you to take an order to the baker. One hundred hot buns. You'll need to wait for him to fill the order so you can bring them back with you. Can you do that for me?"

Jasper nodded eagerly. "Yes, Headmistress!"

The headmistress' lips twitched into a smile beneath her iron-rimmed spectacles. "Take your coat, now. It's chilly out there."

"And the cap?" Jasper asked.

"And the cap."

Jasper snugged the cap onto his head and pulled on his threadbare coat. In no time at all, he was through the rusted gate, his feet flying down the snowy road. There was a new hole in the toe of one of his shoes, and he could feel the snow crusting over it, melting into his sock. But for once, he didn't care. This was his chance.

Jasper slowed himself down just enough to say good morning to Mr. Brewer, the candlemaker, once he got into town.

"Morning, Jasper." The stooped candlemaker eyed the gray sky. "I expect more snow tonight."

"Is that so, Mr. Brewer?" Jasper panted, keeping his own eyes glued on the road ahead. He was nearly to the baker's.

A delivery truck rambled past. Mr. Brewer grunted. "Furniture, I suppose. I hear those Gershams are moving into the Widow Thorne's old house as soon as next week."

There was a touch of sour on Jasper's otherwise cheery mood. "Oh? I hadn't heard."

Mr. Brewer nodded gloomily. "Take care of yourself then, Jasper."

Jasper jogged on toward the baker's but the spring in his step had slowed. "At least he won't be living in their house when Christmas Day comes," he said to himself. Still, he had hoped that the Gershams would find a reason not to stay in the town after all. But moving in made it final.

Jasper kept an eye out for Bess as he dodged through the throngs of people on the snowy sidewalk. When he passed the carpenter's shop, he paused to stare in the window. This was his favorite time of year at the carpenter's shop. Old Mr. Finch made children's toys all year long—spinning tops and wooden airplanes, sets of miniature ninepins with little wooden balls to knock them over. He made dollhouses and cuckoo clocks, rocking horses and little carved elephants, stools and coat stands and trains that ran on wooden tracks.

But when Christmas drew near, Mr. Finch added a whole new collection to his shop window. Out came the jolly, smiling Santas and the nutcrackers with their straight arms and square jaws. Out came the Christmas puppets hanging from their strings, the wooden angels, the reindeer and sleds, complete with tiny wooden boxes Jasper imagined were stuffed with all sorts of tiny gifts.

Jasper could stare into Mr. Finch's windows for long minutes, drinking in the details on every little carving. There was only one thing he could imagine that would make them better. Sometimes, he would squint his eyes and imagine the angels and nutcrackers painted in dazzling blues and golds, the Santas' cheeks dotted with red to match their merry suits.

Today, though, Jasper paused only long enough for a lingering glance before shaking himself and hurrying on to the baker's. There were more important things to do today than stare into the carpenter's window.

Jasper gave the headmistress' order to Mr. Willoughby, who smiled at him and told him to come back in an hour to pick it up.

He waved goodbye to the baker and stepped back out into the snowy square. A flash of red across the way caught his eye. Jasper's heart leapt in his chest. It was the loveliest red scarf he had ever seen, tied around the throat of none other than Bess Shelby. Jasper's first impulse was to race over to her, calling her name, but there was another half of him that kept his feet planted on the sidewalk outside the baker's shop. Would it would be too bold to go over to her? Even rude?

Bess caught sight of Jasper staring at her. She smiled and waved. Jasper grinned in relief. He hurried across the square toward her and was filled with delight when she came toward him, too.

"What are you doing in town?" Bess said when they met in the middle of the square, beside the frozen duck pond. There were no ducks this time of year. They had flown south in autumn.

"An errand for Headmistress Cicely," Jasper said. Bess looked so pretty in her lambswool coat and crimson scarf. He supposed anyone would in such lovely clothes, but with her bright eyes and cheery pink cheeks, Jasper thought there was something naturally beautiful about her. As if even if she were wearing gray, worn out clothes like him, she would still glow a little. Of course, he didn't tell her so.

Instead, he said, "Maybe I could show you the hideout I made in the woods? You could bring Andrew and George too, if you want. Or any of your friends." He hoped Henry Gersham didn't count as one of her friends.

Bess smiled. "I'd love to," she said. Then she added, "But I'm helping my mother hang up Christmas decorations today. Maybe we can go another day."

"Oh. Alright." It was better than a *no*. Jasper remembered all the beautiful Christmas decorations that filled the mayor's house, the lights in blue and white and red and green. He remembered spying through the window on Christmases past, absorbing the sight of a Christmas tree draped in popcorn and tinsel. All the different colors of wrapping paper, the gleaming ribbons and bows. The nativity scenes, the candlelight, the snowmen in the yard.

He almost said something foolish like, "Maybe I can come help you hang up the Christmas decorations?" But he stopped himself. What was he thinking? He was just a dirty orphan boy with a hole in his shoe and a raggedy coat. He had no parents, no gifts to give—he probably wouldn't even know how to hang up Christmas decorations if he tried. And Henry was still staying in the Shelbys' house right now, anyway. No need to give him another reason to mock Jasper.

"I'll see you around," Jasper said, and he hurried away.

Jasper caught himself automatically walking the path back to McCallister's when he remembered that he still had to pick up the buns from the bakery. He must have still had nearly an hour to wait. He didn't think he could go back into town now. If Bess saw him just sitting around in the square while she trimmed the tree or decorated the lawn, she might feel sorry for him. And Jasper wouldn't have that kind of friendship.

Instead, he looked over his should to make sure no one was watching, then ducked down his secret path into the woods.

Chapter 6

irds fat with down feathers flitted in the trees as Jasper picked his way through the brambles to his secret spot. He looked around, then pretended to warm his hands in front of an imaginary fireplace. "The fireplace! Where my stocking shall hang," Jasper said in the snowy silence of the woods. He pretended to hang a large stocking, one with lots of room for toys and candy and with his name painted down the front.

Next, he picked a scraggly birch tree. "A lovelier Christmas tree has never been seen," Jasper announced. Then, he pretended to string it with lights and hung imaginary ornaments on each branch.

"And, of course, a Christmas tree would never be complete without gifts underneath!"

Jasper reached into his pocket to pull out an imaginary gift. As he did, he felt a piece of something sharp. He frowned and pulled out a handful of hard, sticky bits of broken candy cane. The one he had been saving for Bess. Then, he remembered the crunch as Henry had shoved him in the stomach.

Jasper moaned. "I wish just *once* I had a gift to give! I wish someone would leave something for me, in a stocking or under a tree, or even wrapped in an old piece of newspaper. Why does Christmas have to be so *unfair?*"

Just then, Jasper heard a faint ringing of bells. "Hello?" he called. He looked around. No one ever came to this spot, and sound never traveled from the village, either. It was too hidden. His heart beat faster. "Who's there?"

Then, for just a small glimmer of a second, the bare birch tree seemed to glow with color. It looked just as Jasper had imagined, a proud pine tree covered in twinkling lights and colorful ornaments, even an angel on top. But before Jasper could blink, the shimmer vanished, and the tree's bare branches quivered in an eerie wind.

"That wasn't real," said Jasper. He had just been imagining, after all. Perhaps he was letting his imagination get too far. But his breath was catching in his chest and his heart was fluttering. Whatever had just happened really had seemed real, if only for an instant.

Before waiting to see whether anything else would happen, Jasper unfroze himself and went racing through the brambles back down the path he had come. At the edge of the forest, he looked both ways to make sure no one was in sight, then he emerged and brushed off the twig and bark from his pant legs.

"That wasn't real," Jasper quietly chanted with each step down the sidewalk. "Magic's not real."

Jasper watched some of the village children ice skating as he passed the pond on the outskirts of town. In the town square, he saw a pair of horses harnessed to a wagon outside the black-smith's, and the blacksmith himself hefting sacks into the back of the wagon. Each sack seemed to weigh more than Jasper did—but then, Jasper didn't weigh very much.

A cold sting reminded Jasper of the hole in his shoe and the snow melting through it.

He wriggled his toes, trying to keep them warm.

By the time the buttery scent of warm bread reached Jasper, he had forgotten all about the strange moment in the woods.

Chapter
7

"**R**ight on time," Mr. Willoughby said when Jasper opened his door. Its little bell jingled. It reminded him of Christmas bells, which made his heart ache just a little, and then for a fleeting moment, he thought of the jingling sound he had heard in the woods.

"Here you are," the baker said, lifting two bulging sacks of buns onto the counter. Jasper took them, one sack over each shoulder. He lingered a moment to see if the baker would give him a spare bun for his efforts, but it seemed he wasn't so lucky today.

Jasper kicked the baker's door open and propped it with a foot as he scooted outside. When he removed his foot, the door swung shut behind him. He settled the sacks of buns on his shoulders and started down the sidewalk. At the carpenter's shop, he paused to admire a new set of nutcrackers in the window, the wood sanded to a shiny bronze. Two large ones flanked two medium ones, while in the center stood two nutcrackers so small they could have stood on Jasper's open palm.

Jasper looked past the nutcrackers to old Mr. Finch, hunched at his work table inside. The carpenter moved slowly on the other side of the glazed window, his watery eyes bent close to the wooden angel he was carving.

Jasper turned away from the window to head back to the orphanage. But he must have been moving too fast, because right as he turned, he tripped on something and went sprawling into the snow. The sacks of buns flew from his hands and burst open, spilling hot buns into the muddy street. Jasper pushed himself up, rubbing his scraped knees. He looked down at himself, mud-splattered, the knees of his pants torn. He looked at the buns scattered around him in the sludge. A horse cart went clopping by. Its wheels rolled over one of the buns, smashing it into the mud.

Tears stung Jasper's eyes. *Why can't anything happen right for me?* he wondered. *I can't even do something so simple as retrieving hot buns from the baker's. None of the boys will have bread tonight, and it's all because of me.* Jasper swallowed and tried very hard to keep his tears inside as he went about collecting the buns from the street. *It does no good to cry*, he told himself. *You're too old to cry about something small like this.*

As Jasper gathered the buns, doing his best to brush off the snow and mud, he looked around to see what he had tripped on. He noticed a piece of firewood on the sidewalk outside the baker's door. *That wasn't there when I went in,* he thought, frowning. No wonder he had tripped. What was a piece of firewood doing on the sidewalk?

Then, he noticed a slithery path through the snow leading up to the piece of firewood. Jasper heard a snicker. He followed the path of the firewood's slide toward the snicker, and then he saw them— peeking around the corner of the candle-maker's shop was Henry Gersham and a band of his buddies. They snickered again when they saw the look on Jasper's face. Then, Henry pulled the others out of sight. They disappeared around the corner, leaving Jasper standing in the street with buns scattered around him, a half-filled sack drooping glumly from his hand. His face was as red as Santa's fuzzy coat.

It wouldn't be so shameful if I wasn't so easy to make fun of, Jasper thought. He sniffled, pushing very hard against the tears that wanted to come. But he couldn't stop himself from thinking, *How awful it will be to have Henry Gersham living in town.* And even worse—how could Jasper be Bess' friend if Henry lived next door to her? Henry would be able to see her all the time. She wouldn't have enough time or attention left for a raggedy orphan boy who lived all the way outside town.

Jasper was about to let his tears fall, feeling so miserable and sorry for himself that he almost didn't notice that someone had begun picking up the buns from the slushy street. Old Mr. Finch had hobbled out of his carpentry shop and stooped with a sack in one hand, collecting the buns one by one from the mud and snow.

"Mr. Finch!" Jasper exclaimed. "You don't have to help me." He leapt to gather the buns himself. Mr. Finch was far too old to be bending over in the snowy street, picking up buns.

"Nay nay, young sir," the carpenter wheezed. "It's always a pleasure to help when I can."

Jasper didn't argue, and they collected the spilled buns in silence for half a minute before Jasper—who wasn't feeling quite so bad for himself anymore—worked up the courage to ask, "Wouldn't the nutcrackers look much better if they were painted red and green and blue? And wouldn't the little angels look beautiful in gold and white?"

Old Mr. Finch paused to look in the window of his shop. He nodded and sighed, dropping a bun into his sack. "Many years ago," he said, "when I was a young man, I would paint all my carvings myself. Red, blue, green, white, gold—every color. But when I got married and had a family, there was no time to paint the nutcrackers and angels and Santas. I had little children to care for, and they would always spill my paints, or smudge the figurines when the paint was still wet.

My only chance was to paint them after the children had gone to bed, but by then I was too tired from working all day and… well, you know," he said with a twinkle in his eye, "being a father. Takes a lot of time, being a father does. You don't know what you spend most of that time actually *doing*, but it goes somewhere."

The old carpenter tied up his sack and handed it to Jasper. "So the figurines went unpainted. Years passed, and my children grew. I hired my sons to paint my figurines for me, and for years they did. But then they married and started families of their own, and moved away to the city. My dear wife passed away and I became old. My vision isn't what it used to be. I no longer have the energy or the eyesight to paint my figurines."

Mr. Finch grunted as he stepped back up onto the sidewalk and opened the door to his shop. "Of course, if I could find someone young and energetic who was willing to paint my figurines for me…"

Jasper flushed. "I could!" he exclaimed. "Would you let me work for you, Mr. Finch? Would you?"

The old carpenter's eyes sparkled. His wrinkly face smiled. "That just might be grand," he said.

"I'd work hard," Jasper promised. "I'd come every day after my studies! I'm sure the headmistress would let me. If I told her I had a *job*—"

"Tell you what," the old carpenter said. "If you promise to be here tomorrow, I'll go over to the shop and buy some paints this afternoon—red, blue, green, white, gold. When you're done with your work at the orphanage tomorrow, you can come over and paint every figurine you see in the window today. I'll pay you one shilling for every figurine you paint."

One shilling for every figurine. Jasper's eyes went wide at the thought of it. A whole shilling! For every one! He had never earned any money of his own, never *had* any money of his own. He held out his hand with its tattered mitten. "I'll do it, Mr. Finch. I'll work harder than any of your sons!"

Mr. Finch laughed and shook Jasper's hand.

Chapter
8

All that night, Jasper paced in his room practicing what he would say to Headmistress Cicely until Edgar threw a pillow at him. In the morning, Jasper jumped out of bed and walked confidently down to the headmistress' office.

"What do you think, Headmistress Cicely? May I accept the job?" he asked, after explaining everything.

The headmistress sighed. "Goodness knows I can't keep sending you to town for errands," she said. She had had to put the sullied buns outside for the dogs the night before, and Jasper, so used to going unseen, had felt the glares of the other Mackies all through dinner.

But the headmistress must have forgiven him, for although she pressed her lips together seriously, Jasper could see her eyes crinkling at him.

"So long as you keep up with your studies," Headmistress Cicely said at last.

And so the next day, Jasper raced through his arithmetic and his daily reading (which he had finished weeks ago, actually, but the matrons didn't believe him and made him do it again). He raced through a chapter on the history of the Chinese dynasties, which felt so far away and irrelevant to his life that he wondered why the matrons made them read it at all. Oh it was *interesting*, he wouldn't deny that. There were great stories buried in history, often more exciting than made-up stories. But knowing the Tang Dynasty from the Song Dynasty wasn't going to buy him a warmer coat or shoes that wouldn't let in the snow or friends, for that matter. Friends were what he really needed.

When he finished at last, Jasper bade the other orphans a cheery goodbye and ran all the way into town. He presented himself at old Mr. Finch's door, and the old man smiled and said, "Why, Jasper. How pleasant to see you this afternoon."

And thus, his work began.

He was sloppy at painting that first day. It should have been easy to get all the colors to stay in their proper places, he thought. A nutcracker's coat should be green, his belt should be red, his little buttons all gold. But the red seemed to want to run into the green, the green wanted to play tag with the gold, and all the colors ended up smearing into one another and blending into some questionable shades of brown.

When Mr. Finch approached, Jasper worried what he would do when he saw the runny-colored nutcracker. But Mr. Finch didn't scold him. Instead, he gently stepped beside him, took the nutcracker from Jasper's hands with his own hands—which trembled slightly—and showed him. "Like this, see."

The old man showed him how to make slow, smooth strokes with the brush, waiting for each color to dry before adding the next. Anytime Jasper messed up, Mr. Finch would say in his kindly voice, "Like this, see."

Jasper spent that whole first day trying to get one nutcracker right. By the end of the day, that nutcracker's coat was thick from all the layers of mistakes. But his coat was finally green, his buttons gold, and Jasper had even managed to paint the neat little dots of his eyes. And when Mr. Finch handed Jasper that first shilling, Jasper stood as straight and as tall as the nutcracker itself. Jasper turned it over and over in his hand. "It's the first one I've ever owned," he whispered. And it hadn't been handed to him by anyone who felt sorry for him. He had earned it.

"Who knows," said Mr. Finch. "Maybe tomorrow you'll earn two."

Mr. Finch was right. The second day, Jasper painted two – another nutcracker and a snowman.

On the third day, Jasper raced through his morning schoolwork so that he could spend more time at the carpenter's shop. Right away, he picked up a freshly carved angel to work on.

"Ah," said Mr. Finch. "The angels were always my favorite to paint. They look the easiest because they don't have as many colors. But you can give them a lot of character if you put your heart into it."

He showed Jasper how to loosen his grip on the paintbrush and make light strokes. Jasper found that the less he forced it, the more his paintbrush seemed to naturally find just the right shape on its own. When he finished the angel, he cleared a space in the window display and proudly set her there to dry.

Without a word, Mr. Finch gave a small nod. Then, he pulled out a chair for Jasper and shuffled into the back room. When he came out, he set a cup of tea at his seat and handed Jasper a steaming mug of hot chocolate, marshmallows bobbing happily on the top. Jasper gasped.

"Tell me, Jasper," said Mr. Finch, "you have some friends where you live? The schooling is sufficient?"

Jasper gulped. There it was again. A friendly person who wanted to know about his life. Something in Jasper wanted to tell him — about the drafty bunk rooms, the thin blankets, the leaky boots. About the just barely *bearable* sameness day after day. About no Christmas gifts.

He even had a fleeting urge to tell this old man what he had never told anyone before, that all he really wanted was his *real* parents. That what he wanted was to be able to tell them how much he loved them, how he thought of them every day, how he wished sickness hadn't taken them when he was still too young to remember what their faces looked like, how every problem he'd ever had would be solved if only they were here.

That what he wanted was to hug them. Even if just once.

But Jasper looked at the old man smiling as he sipped his tea. *He doesn't really want to know all that,* Jasper decided, just like he had with Bess. *It will only make him feel bad, and feel bad for me.*

So instead, Jasper licked the white foam on his lip and said, "This cocoa is delicious, Mr. Finch. Did you make the very same for your sons?"

The old man took the hint and changed the subject to

himself, and then soon, they sat again comfortably in silence as Mr. Finch carved and Jasper painted. By the end of the day, he had finished three whole figurines, and he thanked Mr. Finch as he dropped the coins into his pocket, pleased with the sound they made as they clanked together.

He waved goodbye and began to wonder what he would do with the shillings he was saving as he walked out the door. "Perhaps I'll by *myself* a birthday gift this year," Jasper thought for a moment. But he knew what he really wanted to buy. Christmas was fast approaching and he would have to work hard, but he set his mind on it. He would buy Bess a Christmas gift.

"Jasper!"

He looked up, and there she was, her cheeks dimpling as she smiled. Jasper blushed, hoping hard that he had not been mumbling his thoughts aloud, as he sometimes did. "Hello, Bess."

Chapter 9

"Isn't this shop wonderful?" Bess asked Jasper, pointing to the carpenter's shop behind him. "Were you looking at Christmas gifts there?"

"Actually, I've just taken a job there," said Jasper with a bubble of confidence. "Painting Mr. Finch's figures."

"You don't mean it!" said Bess. "Did you paint the angel in the window?"

"Mmhm."

"It's just wonderful!" Bess gushed. "Truly, it looks lovely."

Jasper looked down at his feet, trying to hide his triumphant smile. "Do you... do you remember my hideout I told you about in the woods?"

"Yes," said Bess. "I remember."

"Would you like me to show it to you? Perhaps tomorrow afternoon?"

Bess glanced back at her house. "I'm busy tomorrow. With piano practice, and then I'm to help Mother bake Christmas cookies. Sorry, Jasper."

Jasper smiled, because what else could he do, and said, "Goodbye then."

But Jasper ran into Bess coming out of the shop two more times that week, and each time it was the same. Bess had dance class, sewing lessons, and worst of all, plans her mother had made with her "other friends." Jasper had nodded, knowingly, but he couldn't help but wonder whether her mother had really made plans or whether she was making excuses not to play with *him*. And if she was playing with other friends, well, he couldn't help thinking about what separated them from him. What it really came down to, time and again, was money.

Jasper worked hard all that week, and by the end of the week, he had greatly improved in his painting technique and his speed, too. Each night he went home with his pockets a little heavier with shillings clanging together inside. When he got back to McCallister's he would wait until Edgar's breathing grew deep and slow with sleep, and then he would add his new shillings to a sock, which he kept under his thin mattress so that the other boys wouldn't see.

The sock was almost half full already, and Jasper wondered how many shillings it would take for him to buy a nice gift for Bess, one that was as special as she was. Some nights, it would keep him awake, trying to think of the sort of gift he could give her. Other nights, he imagined her smiling as she opened his gift to her, and maybe even giving him a small gift in return. If he imagined very hard, Jasper would fall asleep smiling.

It wasn't just about the money, though. Jasper was enjoying the work, too, and even more, he was enjoying Mr. Finch's simple company. On Friday of that first week, Mr. Finch invited Jasper to stay for dinner, which Jasper gladly accepted. The old carpenter didn't eat as nicely as Mayor Shelby's family, that was for sure. But at least the simple egg sandwich was different than the overcooked vegetables and hard rolls Jasper had been eating his whole life, and Mr. Finch made for more interesting company than the other orphans who shouted and played games as they wolfed down their food.

Saturday morning, Jasper didn't have to rush through his reader or any arithmetic. He pulled on his coat and walked to town through the quiet dawn. When he stepped into the shop, the little bell tinkled as the door swung shut behind him.

Mr. Finch smiled. "Two weeks."

"Two weeks until Christmas!" Jasper agreed happily. He got out his paints from the little cupboard they sat in and began unscrewing their lids. Mr. Finch lined up the day's newly carved figurines for him to paint.

"What are your plans for Christmas?" Mr. Finch asked. He was bent over his work desk, spectacles perched on the tip of his nose, carving away.

"None," Jasper blurted quickly, not wanting to give away even a hint of his best secret, the gift he gave himself each year. But he realized that Mr. Finch might take that 'none' and start feeling sorry for Jasper and feel like he had to invite him over for dinner, even if he didn't want to. Surely his sons and their families would be coming, his real sons, and the thought that Jasper wouldn't belong there, that he would only be there out of pity, that wasn't the sort of Christmas dinner he had dreamed of. "I mean, nothing different than every year," he corrected himself. "You know, they'll serve dinner at the orphanage."

Jasper worked extra hard all that day to take his mind off of his thoughts. He tried to distract himself from wondering whether he should tell Mr. Finch that Christmas was also his birthday or the truth about what Christmas Day was like for him. He tried not to think too hard of Bess and her loving family, her wonderful Christmas presents, her sparkling Christmas tree and delicate crystal angels that he would never have. No matter how much he painted, though, he couldn't help but wonder whether he might still have a chance to have a friend this Christmas. *That's right, don't give up hope*, he thought to himself. *Bess called you a friend, and soon, you will give her a Christmas gift, just like a real friend does.*

He took a break after three hours, when his eyes ached from squinting at red and green and gold paint and his hands were cramped and weary. He stepped outside Mr. Finch's shop and stretched. It was a clear day, and last night's snow lay across the square in a glittering white blanket almost too bright to look at. The snow had been churned to slush where wagon tracks had run through it. In one leafless tree, a robin was warbling.

Jasper caught sight of a red scarf hurrying through the throngs of people, and his heart leapt. He was in luck! He hurried after Bess. When he caught her, he twitched her sleeve, then drew his hand away quickly, afraid he had been too presumptive.

Bess turned in surprise. "Jasper!"

He beamed. "Maybe today?"

Bess looked instantly guilty. "I have piano." She looked down at the parcels she was carrying in her arms. "And I have to take these to the post office."

Christmas gifts being sent away to relatives, no doubt. Jasper looked at them and sighed. "Tomorrow then?" he asked hopefully. "Actually tomorrow?"

Bess looked unconvinced. "Maybe. Hopefully. I don't know, Jasper. I might be busy tomorrow too."

For a moment Jasper wanted her to say it straight out: she didn't want to play in the woods with him, or her parents wouldn't let her, or she didn't like him and wanted him to stop pestering her. For a moment it seemed that would have been better than day after day of *maybe tomorrow*.

But then, Jasper remembered that that was what he had gotten his whole life. He didn't want to be ignored any longer. "Alright," he said, already turning away, feeling ashamed of himself, for himself, for no particular reason. "Well . . . . Let me know."

"I will." Bess smiled and hurried on her way.

Jasper watched her until someone jostled him from behind. He stepped out of the way, apologizing, before he realized it was Henry Gersham.

"Keep trying, painter boy," Henry snickered. He shoved past Jasper and trotted after Bess. When he caught up to her, he offered to carry her parcels for her. She let him.

Jasper watched them chatter happily until they were lost in the crowd.

Chapter 10

J asper felt completely empty. He went back inside the carpenter's shop and picked up a wooden train to paint. He wasn't sure what kept him going, but he worked for four more hours without even taking a break to join Mr. Finch for tea.

The windows outside the shop darkened, and soon the moon reflected off of yesterday's snow. Mr. Finch packed up his things and invited Jasper to join him for dinner, but Jasper thanked him and shook his head. Not tonight. His stomach rumbled, but he wanted to finish at least two more figurines before he stopped.

"Would you be so kind as to close up the shop when you're

done then?" Mr. Finch asked as he picked up his coat from the back of his chair.

Jasper said he would. They bade each other goodnight, and Jasper listened to Mr. Finch's slow footsteps creaking on the stairs as he climbed to his flat above the shop. In the light of a flickering oil lamp, Jasper kept painting. He finished two more figurines and picked up a third.

Snow began falling outside once again, and across the square, the Shelbys' Christmas decorations flickered with lights.

Jasper set his paintbrush down a moment to stare at the full-sized Santa figurine the Shelbys had erected in front of their house. A snowman stood to one side of it, and on its other side was a sleigh with a sack bulging with gifts. With a sigh, Jasper shifted his gaze to the figurines cluttering Mr. Finch's shop window. They stood silhouetted against the Shelbys' lit-up windows across the square. For a moment, Jasper saw them all as soldiers, standing in rank, nutcrackers and Santas and angels frightfully still as they waited for the command to attack.

Jasper rubbed his eyes and looked down at the little lamb half-painted in his hand. *You're tired, Jasper,* he told himself. *You should go to bed.*

There was a creak on the stair. Jasper turned, but the stairwell was dark. His lamp flickered. He looked back to the Santa in the Shelbys' yard across the square. Its head was turned toward him, little glass eyes twinkling above its fluffy white beard. Jasper frowned. Had it been facing him a minute ago?

He shook himself and dipped his paintbrush in the black paint. He touched it carefully to the lamb's tiny hooves. *Maybe just one more,* he thought as he finished the lamb and set it aside. He picked up the carpenter's last carving of the day: an angel with beautiful spread wings and a bell in one hand, raised high as if she were summoning all the children to gather round and enjoy the festivities of Christmas.

Jasper sighed and began painting. White for her wings, gold for the bell, light blue for her dress. He wished someone would summon him to enjoy the festivities of Christmas. He painted in silence for a few minutes. Then, once again, he glanced at the Christmas decorations in the Shelbys' yard. Santa was staring at old Widow Thorne's house next door.

Jasper blinked. Hadn't Santa been looking at *him* a few minutes ago? All of a sudden, he felt uncomfortable in the silence of the carpenter's dark shop. The thought of trudging alone all the way to the orphanage outside town made him shiver. But the thought of staying here, with that moving Santa just across the way, was even worse. Jasper set aside the angel, only half painted, and hurriedly put away the paints. He pulled on his coat and scarf and his boots with the hole in the toe. He locked up Mr. Finch's shop as he had promised he would and ran all the way back to the orphanage.

Chapter 11

When Jasper woke the next day, he laughed at how silly he had been the night before. He wasn't usually such a silly boy. No, he was usually quite level-headed. But there had been something strange about being all alone in Mr. Finch's shop late into the night, with his stomach rumbling and his eyelids drooping as he tried to finish painting the figurines. Sometimes your mind did strange things when you were tired, he knew.

On his way to the carpenter's shop that day—just to be sure—Jasper paused in front of the Shelbys' house. He looked at the Santa. *Just as I thought*, he told himself, and he nodded in satisfaction. Santa was staring happily at Widow Thorne's house next door. Well, the Gersham's house now. There was a jolly smile on his face. Nothing unusual at all.

The door to the Shelbys' house opened and Jasper turned quickly away. He didn't want to be caught staring into the Shelbys' front yard. Bess might think he was lurking around for her (which he partially was, but it was no good if *she* knew that) and if it was Mrs. Shelby... well, Mrs. Shelby didn't seem to like him much. Whenever she caught sight of him talking to Bess, her lip gave that little twitch, the same sort of twitch that happens when you step in dog poo in the street.

"Hey, Jasper!" a voice called. "Grubby Jasper!"

Jasper knew Henry Gersham's voice by now. He shouldn't have turned, but he did. Henry was coming out the Shelbys' front door with Bess. He was grinning, ruddy, dressed in a smart tweed jacket with brass buttons. Jasper felt a stab of jealousy. *What's Henry been doing in the Shelbys' house? They already moved out.*

"Scram, you little street rat!" Henry called, making a shooing motion with his hand. "Go back to grubbing around in the gutt—"

"Henry!" Bess smacked his arm. "Cut it out!"

Henry looked at her in genuine surprise, as if he had thought he was pleasing her by calling Jasper names. "You don't want him gaping around your yard, do you? He's cracked, you know. Turning into one of those little nutcrackers he makes," he said, cackling at his own joke.

Bess scowled. "You're a right bully, Henry Gersham. Go on. You leave. I don't want you to walk me to my dance lessons."

"But—"

"I said I *don't want it*!" She looked about ready to smack him again, so Henry took the clue and huffed his way down the path toward the gate at the front of the yard. Only he didn't reach the gate. Instead, he on the front of Santa's sleigh and went sprawling in the snow.

Henry leaped up, red-faced with indignation. "That stupid thing moved!" he shouted, thrusting a finger at Santa's sleigh. "I swear it *moved* to trip me!"

"Don't be daft now, Henry," Bess snapped. "Coming up with excuses only makes you look silly. Go on, get out of my yard."

Henry straightened his nice tweed jacket as he stomped to the gate. It was covered in snow and all rumpled, Jasper was pleased to see. Henry threw open the gate and flounced past Jasper. Jasper was expecting a push, but with Bess watching from the front step, Henry didn't dare.

Jasper didn't know what to say to Bess, as much as he wanted to say something. So, he gave her a grateful smile and left for Mr. Finch's shop. He worked industriously all afternoon, painting figurine after figurine until his hands cramped and Mr. Finch told him he'd better go for a walk before his head started aching, too. Jasper was pleased that Mr. Finch was concerned for him, but he said, "I'll be alright, Mr. Finch. I can go another hour." And he kept on painting.

The hour was only halfway up when the little bell on the carpenter's shop door rang. Jasper was in the middle of painting a nutcracker. He looked up to see Bess Shelby push her way into Mr. Finch's shop. She was smiling. It was such a lovely sight that Jasper leapt from his chair, nearly spilling his paints. "Bess!"

She looked curiously at the nutcracker he was painting. "I'll be free tomorrow," she said. "Maybe we can explore the woods together? My little brother George wants to come, too."

"Yes!" Jasper cried eagerly. "Yes."

"Lovely. And you won't mind George?"

"No," Jasper said, flattered that she was asking. "Not at all."

She looked happy, genuinely happy. "I'm sorry it took so long," she said. "I've been looking forward to it!"

Jasper was so flushed with happiness he didn't know what to say. His cheeks got all red and he stammered something that probably sounded truly dumb.

"That's a lovely nutcracker," Bess said. She glanced around the shop, admired an angel, giggled at a Santa, then said, "Alright then. I'll see you tomorrow." She turned for the door.

Jasper tried to think of something to say. He wanted to promise her that it would be the best time she had ever had, better than ballet lessons or piano practice or her *other friends*. But he didn't want to sound arrogant or silly, so all he said was, "See you tomorrow."

The rest of that day, the paintbrush moved in Jasper's hand as if it had a mind of its own. It danced over the wood, moving to the sound of his whistling. When he got up for a snack with Mr. Finch, he practically danced about the shop.

"What has you so tickled?" the old carpenter asked.

"I'm going to play in the woods tomorrow with Bess!" Jasper cried.

Mr. Finch's eyes twinkled. "This has been an achievement long in the pursuing, I take it?"

"Oh, *so* long Mr. Finch! I thought she'd never have the time. But after tomorrow, we'll be proper friends, I'm convinced of it!"

"Playing in the woods makes *proper friends?*" Mr. Finch asked as he ate a cracker with cheese.

"It's one of the things that makes proper friends, yes." Jasper's eyes shone. "What luck I've had!" He snatched up a painted Santa and kissed it. "It's Santa's Christmas gift to me!" As the words came out of his mouth, he suddenly remembered another gift: the one he had planned to buy for Bess, to show her that he was serious about being her friend. *I need to pick it out!* he thought frantically. *I need to have something to give her tomorrow! And something for George, too!*

Jasper thought about the sock that was now stuffed with shillings, carefully tucked under his mattress back at the orphanage. He looked around Mr. Finch's shop. Bess had said the nutcracker he was painting was *lovely.* Then, he remembered how she had admired the angel in the window, the one he had painted on just his third day of working at the shop. But when he picked it up now, he could feel that it was a bit globby in some places. His work had gotten much neater and smoother since then.

Finally, a Santa figurine grinned at him from the corner. Even though Jasper had painted its eyes himself, they almost seemed to be glistening at him, the shining red mouth practically turning up at the corners on its own.

This is my chance. I must not waste it. "May I run to the orphanage really quickly?" Jasper asked Mr. Finch. "I'll be back in twenty minutes, I promise."

The old carpenter smiled and brushed the cracker crumbs from his hands. "Of course."

Just as he had promised, Jasper was back in twenty minutes with his sock full of coins. "I want to buy this Santa," he announced, panting.

"Now, Jasper, don't be silly," Mr. Finch said. "That must be nearly all your savings. And besides, you painted that Santa yourself. In the spirit of Christmas, please, take it."

Jasper swallowed hard. It was tempting, to have the Santa and a sock full of shillings beneath his mattress, too. But he shook his head.

"I've never bought a gift for anyone before. I've always wanted to, but I've never been able to. Please, Mr. Finch, I would like to buy this Santa."

So, Mr. Finch picked up the charming Santa from the window shelf. He wrapped it in old newspaper and handed it to

Jasper, who handed over his carefully saved money, every shilling of it.

That night, he fell asleep happy. He wondered if this was what it meant to have a friend—to have someone say, "See you tomorrow," and know that they actually would.

Chapter 12

The next day, Monday, was the first day of the winter vacation. Usually, early mornings for Jasper were magical, when all the other boys were still sleeping and the world felt like it was just his. But today, even though Jasper jumped out of bed the moment light his the window, Edgar was already pulling on a sweater. The hallways were bustling with boys preparing to turn the crisp new layer of snow into a battlefield of snowballs. Jasper just pushed his way right through. Now that he had a job, he no longer had to sneak his way out of McCallisters.

Jasper didn't go to work in Mr. Finch's shop that morning, though. Instead, gripping the Santa he had bought—still carefully wrapped in the newspaper—he walked past Mr. Brewer

and the bakery and into the town square for Bess. He whis-
tled as he waited, admiring the merry Christmas scene in Bess'
front yard. There was the human-sized Santa with his sleigh
and reindeer, made of wood and wire with little lights twinkling. Beside him was the snowman, looking smart in his black
top-hat. On the other side of the path was a nativity scene
with a glorious angel. A giant gingerbread man peeked out
from behind a tree.

I wonder what gingerbread tastes like, Jasper thought. He
had never tried it.

Soon, Jasper got tired of standing, and sat on a rock outside
the Shelbys' fence. He watched the wagons rattling through
the square. He waited and waited. Bess and George still didn't
show up. Jasper began to fret. What if Bess had said the day
after tomorrow? What if she had said to meet somewhere else?
He would look like a fool for forgetting.

After a bit, Jasper got up and opened the Shelbys' front gate.
He looked at the regal front door and hesitated, then walked
up the path. *I'll just knock and see what happens,* he thought.

But halfway up the path, he stopped himself. He imagined Mrs. Shelby opening the door. He didn't want to see that
look she got on her face whenever she spotted him, like someone had let a mangy dog into the house. *Better not to knock,*
he thought.

To distract himself, Jasper poked around the Christmas scene in the Shelbys' front yard. He checked to see what was in Santa's sack (sawdust, unfortunately, and empty wooden boxes) and picked snow from Santa's fuzzy beard. He thought Santa looked grateful that someone was tending to the state of his beard.

An hour passed. Jasper once again grew tired and this time sat down on the side of Santa's sleigh. He carefully unwrapped the Santa figurine he had bought for Bess and George. He studied it until he grew bored.

He waited another hour. Bess and her brother still didn't come. Jasper paced in the front yard. "I was a fool to think I had a friend," he murmured, then chided himself for jumping to conclusions. Something must have come up, some reason why Bess couldn't play with him. He thought again of knocking, but what if Bess opened the door and told him she had changed her mind about playing? What if she had been inside watching him from a window this whole time?

It was a horrible thought. Jasper sighed and wrapped the Santa figurine back in its newspaper, which was by now rather damp from the snow and the misty air.

Nearly the whole day had passed now, and winter's early darkness was already beginning to settle in. Feeling very alone, Jasper made the long trek back to the orphanage alone. He unwrapped the Santa figurine and set it in the little alcove beside his bed. It was hard not to feel a little less lonely then, with that Santa smiling back at him.

That night, he stared at it as he lay in his bed, listening to the other boys snoring softly in the bunks around him. He thought of Henry Gersham tripping on Santa's sleigh and shouting, "That stupid thing moved! I swear it moved to trip me!"

Jasper's lips twitched into a smile. Wouldn't that be the funniest thing, if Santa *had* actually tripped Henry Gersham?

But a moment later his smile faded, and he found tears on his cheeks instead. Jasper buried his face in his pillow so no one would hear him crying. He had spent his hard-earned money to buy a gift for his new friends, and they hadn't even come.

"Morning, young Jasper," said Mr. Brewer as Jasper tromped through the snow toward Mr. Finch's shop the next morning. "Did you hear the news?"

"What's that?" asked Jasper.

"That Shelby girl. She came down ill yesterday, real suddenly."

"She did? I mean, is she alright?" Jasper asked.

Mr. Brewer shook his head grimly. "She's got the fever, they say. Real bad she's got it."

"Oh," was all Jasper could say. "Oh."

He walked into the square, but instead of going into the shop, he stopped to sit on a stoop.

"The poor doll," a pair of ladies in the square said. "Stuck in her bed and not able to eat but broth and tea, and so close to the holidays."

Mr. Brewer's words echoed in Jasper's mind: *Read bad she's got it.* Jasper pictured the mayor's daughter, pale and feverish, and he felt sorry for her. He hoped she was going to be alright. At the same time, although he knew it was selfish, it did make him feel a little better, knowing that there was a good reason Bess hadn't come to play with him. She would have come if she had been well, he was sure. She couldn't be blamed for falling ill.

There was still a small part of him, though, that wondered how hard it would have been for her to send George out to explain, so that he wouldn't have had to wait the whole day in the Shelbys' front yard, but he shouldn't be mad at her for that. She had a fever and perhaps she had slept all day, perhaps her mind hadn't been clear enough to remember that Jasper would be waiting for her.

Finally, Jasper stood and went into Mr. Finch's shop.

Mr. Finch smiled. "So you have a proper friend now, Jasp?"

Jasper half smiled at the nickname Mr. Finch had taken to calling him, but then he solemnly shook his head. "She fell ill yesterday, it turns out."

"Did she? Sorry about that. I hadn't heard." After a silent moment, Mr. Finch added, "Missed you around here yesterday. There's plenty for you to paint today."

Jasper wasn't sure whether Mr. Finch just meant that he'd gotten used to Jasper's extra set of hands in the shop or that he actually missed Jasper, as something like a friend. But Jasper rolled those words around in his head as he worked. He'd never been missed by anyone, as far as he knew.

At the end of the day, Jasper packed up his paints and Mr. Finch dropped eleven shillings into his palm. "You can start filling that sock up again, seems," Mr. Finch said. "See you tomorrow then."

Jasper left the shop and lingered in the square, trying to get a glimpse of Bess through the windows of the Shelbys' mansion. *A friend would knock on the door and send their well wishes, wouldn't they?* he wondered. But he imagined Mrs. Shelby opening the door, the look on her face when she saw that she had been pulled away from tending to her sick daughter to answer the door for a pestering orphan. Maybe she would even think he was there to beg for money and shut the door in his face before he could say that he hoped Bess would get well soon. He dug his cold hands deeper into his pockets and headed back to McCallister's.

When Jasper walked into the orphanage, he saw a set of parents standing awkwardly with Headmistress Cicely. He knew what that meant, and he quickly swallowed down any hope before it bubbled up inside him.

"That's the one," they said. "Of course, we're hoping he can come to his new home in time for Christmas."

Jasper followed their pointing finger. It went right past him. It was pointing to the little boy, Robin, who hadn't gotten any skates the day of the delivery. The boy looked overwhelmed now, like he was stuck somewhere between absolute glee and panic.

"He's a very nice boy," Headmistress Cicely confirmed. "I believe you'll be a wonderful fit for each other. Let me just speak with him now."

She kneeled down beside the boy and spoke to him gently, and his face shifted into a smile, then an eager nod.

"Would you like to go with them today, or would you like some time to pack up and say goodbye to your friends?" she asked.

Robin laughed. "I haven't got much, it'll only take a minute," he said, and he started to dart off to his room.

Even in his excitement, though, he paused when he noticed Jasper. "Hey," he said. "Thanks again. You know, for the skates."

Jasper nodded. "You're welcome."

"I've got to go," the small boy said, and he glanced back at the couple waiting for him. "Goodbye!"

As Robin fled to his bunk, Jasper imagined him waking up on Christmas morning in his new home, opening gifts from this quiet, smiling couple in the doorway. He was jealous, of course, but this time, he was happy for the boy being adopted, too.

When Jasper climbed into bed that night, he picked up the wooden Santa in the alcove, and he made a decision. "Who cares what her parents think?" he whispered. "Tomorrow, I'll bring my friend a Christmas gift."

"What?" said Edgar through the darkness.

"Nothing," said Jasper.

Chapter 14

The next morning, Jasper picked up the wrapped wooden Santa and set out for town. It was an especially clear morning, beautiful, but the cold was biting. And since Jasper was carefully carrying the Santa, he couldn't even dig his hands into his pockets for extra warmth. These days, his fingers were numb even in the shop, where Mr. Finch's small fireplace and tiny bits of wood weren't enough to keep his fingers from becoming clumsy with cold as he painted. And now, they stung with the frozen morning. And yet, he had spent his money on a gift instead of on a new pair of snug mittens.

When he made it to the Shelby mansion, instead of pausing at the iron gate, he made himself push it open before he could hesitate and turn back. He kept his eyes on the noble front door as he walked past the snowman, the Santa with his saw-dust-filled gifts and his sleigh. Even so, a memory of that Santa staring at him through the carpenter's shop window flashed through him. *I was tired that night,* he reminded himself. *I was seeing things.*

After what felt like an endlessly long walk to the front door, Jasper finally stood before it. He shifted the wrapped Santa to his left hand and reached for the door knocker with his right.

"Don't you dare, you little weasel."

Jasper jumped so hard he nearly fell backwards. "He—Henry."

Henry Gersham stood on the balcony of the house next door, looking down on Jasper in the Shelbys' yard. He looked smart in a stiff wool jacket, blue plaid, with a matching plaid cap on his head. His green eyes were cold.

"You can't just go up to anyone's house, you know," Henry sneered. "I saw you sitting out here the other day. That's called trespassing. And if I catch you do it again, I'll call the police on you. Or better yet, the dogcatcher."

"Please, Henry, I was just—"

"It's probably your fault she got sick anyway," Henry interrupted. "You and your filthy hands, your filthy breath, always hovering around her."

Jasper's cheeks burned with fury, and he wished he could tell him how wrong he was, how just because he had gotten lucky in life didn't make him any better than anyone else. But just then, Henry pelted a snowball off of the balcony. Before Jasper could react, it smashed the Santa he was holding right out of his hands and onto the ground.

"You heard me," Henry called after him. "I said get out of here!"

Jasper scrambled to pick up the Santa and ran clumsily out of the Shelbys' yard. He didn't stop until he was on the other side of the door to the carpenter's shop.

"Why Jasper, my boy. What's happened?" the old man asked, setting down his paring knife.

Suddenly, Jasper felt his eyes sting as the cruelty of what had just happened set in. A wave of thoughts flooded over him. He had only wanted to give a Christmas gift. But maybe Henry was right. Maybe orphans are just not meant to be friends with mayors' daughters. And what if Henry was also right that Jasper had been the reason Bess got sick? No, it couldn't be. Jasper had hardly even had a chance to spend any time with Bess at all. And besides, he wasn't sick himself. He was at least smart enough to know that not all of the terrible things people thought about Mackies were true. But this was then followed by an even worse realization. What if Henry meant what he said about calling the police? How would Jasper get to visit the Shelbys' home on Christmas to watch them celebrate and make his wish, like he did every year?

Jasper couldn't stop himself now. He sat down on the floor and cried.

"Now, now," said Mr. Finch. "It's nothing a little wood glue can't fix."

Jasper gasped. He hadn't even realized that the wooden Santa he was holding had lost the toes of one boot when it thumped against the icy front steps. *Just like my boots*, thought Jasper.

The rest of the morning, Jasper sat by the small glow of a fire sipping tea while Mr. Finch shaped and sanded a new boot for the Santa. He had been so busy painting that it had been a while since he had watched the old man work. It was calming, the way his hands smoothed over the wood.

"There now," said Mr. Finch. "You can just dab a little black paint on there, and it'll be good as new."

As they ate lunch together, they watched through the window as a black automobile pulled up the the Shelby's driveway. A tall, dark man in a long dark coat stepped out. He carried his black doctor's case through the Shelbys' gate, up their front steps, and into their splendid mansion.

"I suppose it's become quite serious," Mr. Finch said over his sandwich. "Poor thing. And I imagine you're worried about her."

Jasper nodded. He was glad that Mr. Finch didn't add something cheery like 'She'll be alright, you'll see.' He hated when adults pretended everything was fine. It wasn't like they were fooling him. Things had never been especially fine in his life.

The black automobile stayed parked in front of the Shelbys' house all that day, and when Jasper left the shop that night, it looked as though it were sleeping there, guarding the gate and all of the jolly Christmas decorations inside it. He looked down at the Santa in his hands, grinning up at him even though it had lost a foot just that morning.

Jasper pressed his lips together. "What are you so jolly about, anyway?"

15

"Been a while since we've seen you, Jasper," said Headmistress Cicely. "Busy working man."

Jasper shrugged, but he was secretly glad that someone had noticed he had been gone, even if it was the headmistress, whose job it was to keep track of all the boys.

"Why don't you stay back with us just for today?" she said. "We're going to the pond again. I'll make sure you get a chance to ice skate this time."

Jasper hesitated. He hoped that Mr. Finch wouldn't worry about him.

"You can go to work after," said the headmistress, as though she were reading his thoughts. And so Jasper pulled on his thin coat and walked with the crowd of boys shouting and pulling each other into the snow.

It was just ten days until Christmas, now, and the town seemed alive with twinkling lights and Christmas carols. Jasper pulled on a borrowed pair of skates, which were loose and wobbly even when he tied them tight. He remembered the feeling of that day when the delivery had come, those few minutes of wearing skates that fit tight, that were his very own. He stepped out onto the ice, and soon, he was gliding easily in circles with the crowd. Even though the breeze was icy cold on his cheeks, it did feel exhilarating to move so quickly and easily.

But of course, being at the pond reminded him of the day that he threw snowballs with Bess, and that she called him a friend. Of course, he still held out hope that Bess would be his friend. But Jasper decided that he would even give that up if it would make Bess well again.

Then Jasper saw the flash of blue plaid jacket and red hair. He didn't even think twice. He glided right to the edge of the pond, untied the ice skates, handed them to Headmistress Cicely, and tromped off to the carpenter's shop before Henry Gerhsam could notice he was there. Now, it seemed, Henry didn't even need to see Jasper to ruin his fun.

"Was wondering if you'd be coming around today," Mr. Finch said when Jasper arrived mid-afternoon.

"Of course, Mr. Finch," said Jasper. They sat in silence for some time, then Jasper spoke up again. "Mr. Finch, I was wondering. Will… will you still need me and all when Christmas is over?"

It was a frightening thought, that Mr. Finch might not need him. He'd grown used to his long afternoons working alongside the old man, sharing the occasional conversation, listening to the rasp of the carpenter's tools as he worked. He'd grown used to the smell of wood dust and cut evergreen, and the more subtle undertones of cinnamon and cloves that always hung about Mr. Finch's age-old furniture. Mr. Finch was almost like… no, Jasper did not dare to compare him to family. He had seen too many people come and go in his life to do that.

"No more Santas and angels and nutcrackers," the carpenter nodded with a knowing smile. "But don't worry. There will be other toys to make the rest of the year. Spinning tops and wooden dolls." He brushed the wood dust from his work table. "You can paint tops and dolls just as easily as Santas and snowmen, can't you? Perhaps I'll even teach you how to sand and polish them, too. Take some work off these old hands."

"That would be grand, Mr. Finch," Jasper said in relief.

Mr. Finch's eyes crinkled as he smiled. "Truth is," he said, sitting down with a *huff* behind his work table, "I would miss you terribly if you stopped coming."

Jasper didn't know what to say to that. They were beautiful words, maybe the most beautiful words anyone had ever said to him. Too beautiful for him to say anything back. So instead, he cleared his own work space without saying anything.

At the orphanage that night, Jasper lay beneath his thin blanket staring at the Santa figurine now back in the alcove beside his bed. He thought about how glad he was that his work with Mr. Finch wouldn't end with Christmas. But then thoughts crept in of Henry Gersham. That one boy was keeping him away from his only friend, and now he might even stand in the way of Jasper's Christmas tradition. Chrismas was just ten days away. What would he do?

As tears rolled down his cheeks, he remembered all the names Henry had called him, that he was a dirty little orphan that had made Bess sick, that he was cracked like the nutcrackers he painted. In his sleep that night, Jasper dreamed that the Santa figurine was evil. It came alive and turned him into a nutcracker, just like Henry Gersham had predicted. In the dream, he discovered that he had wooden limbs and a hinged jaw. The other children drove him from the orphanage with snowballs and stones, screaming, "Nutcracker! Nutcracker! Nutcracker!"

Chapter 16

With just a week left before Christmas, the black car remained in front of the Shelbys' gate. Jasper had almost grown accustomed to the site of it, as though it were part of their Christmas display. He would see the doctor coming and going, his shoulders hunched, always a worried look on his brow.

But now, the talk of the town was beginning to change.

"They say her fever's finally broke," the candlemaker told Jasper as he walked to the carpenter's shop. Jasper felt a flicker of warmth through the frigid air. "Thought you ought to know. You seemed awful worried when I told you she was sick."

"Thank you, Mr. Brewer. That is good news."

"They say she's got a long road of recovery ahead. Still weak as a newborn lamb, I hear. But the doctor thinks she's going to make it," Mr. Brewer said knowingly.

Jasper could almost see the relief in his cloudy breath. Despite Henry Gersham's warnings, Jasper walked just a little nearer to the Shelbys' mansion than he normally did and peered in their large windows. He could see that, for the first time since she had fallen ill, Bess was out of her sickbed. He could just glimpse her propped up on a chair in the front room, covered in thick blankets and with the doctor by her side. Her face looked pale and thin in the twinkling lights of the Christmas tree.

"I wonder if she remembers," Jasper muttered. "Maybe now that she's feeling a bit better, maybe she'll send word to me to visit her. Or send me a letter explaining why she didn't come to play."

He knew deep down that it was too much to hope for just yet, though. It was clear that Bess still wasn't well. He slunk into the carpenter's shop and plopped onto his stool.

"It's the busiest week of the year!" said Mr. Finch merrily. "We'll have to work extra hard these next few days."

And indeed, he was right. All day as he painted, townspeople popped in to buy little wooden Christmas trees, dolls and trains. Jasper had begun to help out with the sales so that Mr. Finch could keep carving. Most of the time, he would jump up and wipe his hands on his apron. He would smile kindly as he handed people their change. But Jasper also recognized which customers held up their chins as they walked in and knew that they might scowl or even walk out of the store if he were to offer them help. Then, he called on Mr. Finch before they even had a chance to look down their noses at him.

Jasper stayed late at the shop that night, and he brought home a pocketful of shillings that made the sock under his mattress again bulge with the coins. Now, he was working more to help Mr. Finch, not because there was something he wanted to buy, but he Jasper began about what to do with them all. He felt a sense of pride as he felt the heaviness of the sock.

I could buy myself Christmas dinner, Jasper thought. *Or one of those nice furry hats in the window of the tailor's shop. Or a thick green scarf like Henry Gersham wears.* But he didn't want Henry to think he was trying to challenge him, so he decided against the scarf. He would know when the right thing came along, he decided.

The next morning, Jasper woke up early to get to Mr. Finch's shop and begin painting. During the day as he worked, he watched all the happy people running around the square through Mr. Finch's shop window. Parcels under their arms, bags overflowing with ribbons and bows. Soon, there would be wrapping to be done, a lot of wrapping. Jasper felt a pang in his chest. He would like to wrap a gift, just once. That seemed a special part of Christmas, wrapping gifts.

When he stepped out of the store for a breath of fresh air that afternoon, he couldn't believe what he saw. A chair was sitting on the front step, and behind it, Mayor Shelby carried Bess in his arms. He arranged the daughter in the chair, and Andrew Shelby appeared in the doorway with a bundle of warm blankets, which he wrapped around her. Between her thick hat and her woolly scarf, only Bess's eyes were showing to watch the snow fall, but even just that sliver of her face looked pale. Jasper watched for a moment, frozen.

Mayor Shelby patted his son's shoulder and retreated inside, and Andrew stood beside his sister in silence for a moment. Jasper kept hoping she might look his way and raise her hand up in a wave. Or even under her thick scarf, she might just smile at him. He would know for sure if she did. But she didn't. She just watched the snow without looking out at the people.

After a moment, another face appeared in the doorway. Henry Gersham carried a steaming mug and handed it to Bess. Then, he looked right at Jasper.

"Go away, mongrel!" Even though Jasper was across the street, in front of the shop where he worked and belonged, the freckle-faced boy made him feel like he had done something wrong.

He lingered a moment to see if Bess would say something to Henry, lift a hand, anything. Instead, she turned to Andrew and said, in the weakest, trembling voice, "The snow is beautiful, isn't it?"

She didn't even look his way. Jasper turned and went back into the shop.

Chapter 17

"I just don't understand," Jasper told Mr. Finch. "She was strong enough to talk. 'The snow is beautiful, isn't it?' That's what she said. So why couldn't she have said something to me?"

"Be patient," said Mr. Finch. "She's sick, after all."

"I thought she was my friend. But she didn't even look my way."

Mr. Finch didn't look up from the wooden rocking horse he was carving. He grunted and pursed his old, leathery lips. "You know," he said at last, "Bess is just a little girl herself." For several seconds, there was only the scrape of his file on the wood. "Just because she has everything she could possibly want, it doesn't make her perfect. Like all people, sometimes she might forget the most valuable things."

Jasper painted in silence for a while, mulling over the old man's words. *Bess is just a little girl herself.*

Andrew had already carried her back inside, and when Jasper looked out the window now, he saw only the mysterious snowman and Santa standing in the yard. They looked, Jasper thought, like they were keeping a secret. And there was something so... *alive* looking about them. It wasn't that they were realistic necessarily. Mr. Finch's figures looked more realistic than those. It was something about their faces, like they weren't quite as stiff or still as the little wooden figurines in the shop. But that was impossible, of course they were still. They were decorations.

Jasper again worked until late that evening. "You should go to bed too, Mr. Brewer," he said.

"Yes," said the old man rubbing his eyes. "I suppose you're right." But the old man didn't stop moving his lathe over the ball of wood in his hand. "Goodnight, Jasper."

Jasper walked home slowly that night. Snow was falling silently, but it was picking up speed. Jasper could almost see it collecting on the ground, getting higher. *If it falls like this all night, we'll be up to our chins in it*, thought Jasper. But there was something thrilling about it. It was soft and gentle but so powerful all at once. It seemed almost magical.

Because the snow was building up so fast, Jasper had to push hard against the rusted gate with the *McCallister's Orpha* sign dangling off of it. It occurred to Jasper that lately the orphanage had simply become the place where he slept at night. He hadn't spoken to the other boys in days, or even the matrons. He just got up and left in the morning, then came in quietly past the others already asleep in their beds, which is just what he did tonight.

As he crawled into he covers, he watched the snow seem to pour down out the window. He looked at the wooden Santa beside him and realized with a start that the next day would be Christmas Eve.

"You know," he whispered, "maybe I will ask Mr. Finch if I can join him for Christmas dinner. *Then* I'll go over and watch the Shelby's open gifts. And make my Christmas wish. Henry Gersham is not going to stop me."

When Jasper woke up in the morning, snow piled up to the bottom of the window, and it was still coming down. He quickly pulled on his coat and boots and headed for the door.

"Not sure if you're going to make it into town today, Jasper," said Headmistress Cicely. "The snow's piled up against the door."

"Besides, it's Christmas Eve!" Matron Simmons smiled. "Give yourself a day off."

Jasper didn't want to take a day off, though. Especially not Christmas Eve. So, he grabbed a shovel and helped a few of the matrons and other boys clear a path from the doorway. Then, he made his way into town, heaving himself through the mounds of snow. He didn't see Mr. Willoughby in the bakery or even Mr. Brewer selling candles.

By the time Jasper arrived at the shop, it was nearly noon. The sidewalks and streets had been cleared by the village workers, although the snow was already beginning to build up again. The lights were off inside the shop, which was strange, and the front door was locked, which was even more unusual. *Must be closed because of the snow,* thought Jasper. *I don't suppose many customers would come in a snowstorm like this, even if it is Christmas Eve.*

He pounded on the door until it finally clicked open. It was only then that Jasper realized that the wooden toys and figurines were not in the window.

"Come on," said Mr. Finch, and he shuffled back to his work table and slumped on the stool. The room was dim. No candles were lit, and the fireplace was cold. The old carpenter's woodworking tools were lined up on his work table in front of him. One by one, he took each tool and tucked it into a battered suitcase.

"What are you doing?" Jasper asked in horror.

"Jasper," Mr. Finch said in a heavy voice, "I got some bad news today. The landlord told me that the rent will go up the first of January. I don't have the money to pay for it, Jasper. I have no choice. I'm going to the city to live with my son." He trailed off, dejected, as he lowered more tools into the battered suitcase.

"But you love carpentry," Jasper protested.

Mr. Finch turned to look at him for the first time, smiling sadly. "Yes, I do. But what am I supposed to do? I don't make enough money with carpentry."

"You're the only friend I have!" Jasper exclaimed.

Mr. Finch's smile turned even sadder. He bowed his head and finished putting the last of his tools into the suitcase. Not knowing what else to do, Jasper miserably helped the old carpenter pack up his things. Then, he went and sat at his stool by the window, facing out so that Mr. Finch wouldn't see him crying.

When he wiped his eyes and saw the snow still piling up,

he brightened just a little. "Mr. Finch," he said, "the snows are too deep for you to travel all the way to the city. And it's still snowing! The roads must be dangerous."

Mr. Finch was sitting behind his work bench, also gazing out the window. He looked as if he didn't know what to do now that there were no more figurines to be carved. "Perhaps you're right, Jasper. It's a long way to the city, and there's no telling how long this snow will continue."

"You'll wait until it stops then? Until the roads clear?"

Mr. Finch rubbed his tired old face. "I'll wait. Would you like some tea?"

And so they sat silently together, sipping tea and watching the snow pile up. Jasper threw a small log in the fireplace and lit a match to it, but the piled up snow kept the drafts from creeping under the door. The weather didn't seem to want Mr. Finch to leave any more than Jasper did.

Jasper knew that eventually the snow *would* stop, and Mr. Finch *would* leave. But for now, he was still here, and that made Jasper happy.

Chapter 18

Then, there it was. Christmas again.

Jasper lay in bed watching the snow swirl by the window, thinking, *I'm nine years old now.* It seemed very old. Eight had seemed old last year. Around June or July, eight had begun to feel right, comfortable, like a well-worn shoe. He had just gotten used to that comfortable feeling, but here was Christmas again, and he was nine now. It would be several more months before nine had that well-worn shoe feeling.

Christmas Day passed slow and dark. The matrons had insisted that he stay at the orphanage that day since the snowstorm was just too strong, and besides, it was Christmas so he wouldn't need to work. At least he knew that Mr. Finch wouldn't be leaving today - the snow all but covered the windows, and it still hadn't stopped.

It seemed a long, dreary time until night fell. The matrons did serve a special Christmas supper this year. Even if it wasn't much, it was different. Hot buns with gravy, mashed potatoes and a candy cane for every child. The gravy was special, and the candy canes. Jasper ate his in silence, alone. He waited until the matrons began clearing the dishes away, then he slipped up to his room for his coat and scarf. He pulled on his shoes (they hadn't gotten any newer, and the hole in the toe was bigger than it had been in November) and snuck out of the orphanage.

He hadn't had to sneak out in a long time, since he'd been coming and going freely to the carpenter's shop. Now, the feeling of sneaking through the somber spruces that crowded the orphanage drive felt nostalgic, and he savored it even if it was much harder pulling himself over the tall drifts of snow. He stepped easily over the rusted gate, mostly buried, and could not see the battered wooden sign that read: *McCallister's Orpha*.

The Shelby's house looked somehow even more majestic than normal rising out of the heavy snow, glowing with different colored lights and trimmed with pine garlands. Jasper had to dig down through the snow to be able to see in the window, and now he lay on his stomach on the snow, peering through that firelit rectangle at the lovely scene inside. It was the same as it had been every year since he could remember. A splendid

Christmas tree all decked in lights, Christmas ornaments nestled between those evergreen needles. Candles flickering, bows and ribbons and steaming hot chocolate. Jasper couldn't help the smile that spread across his face.

His eyes found Bess immediately. Amid the colorfully decorated Christmas tree and gifts of all different sizes and shapes with frilly bows and gleaming ribbons sat Bess, propped up in a sickbed beside the fire, so pale and thin that he hardly recognized her as the bright-eyed, golden-curled girl who'd thrown snowballs at the ice skaters on the pond last month. Still, there was life in her eyes, he could see it.

More careful than ever not to make a sound, Jasper covered his mouth with his hands to stifle his cry of delight as George Shelby unwrapped a kit to build his own train with its own set of tracks. Jasper barely had time to admire the gleaming train— it looked so proud in red and black—before the Shelbys' older son, Andrew, tore the paper off his own gift. The paper fell away to reveal a gleaming leather saddle.

Jasper's eyes bulged. He had always wanted to learn how to ride. He rolled in the snow with excitement as Andrew Shelby grinned. Jasper imagined that *he* had unwrapped the saddle instead of Andrew. He would learn how to ride! He would go as fast as the wind! He almost laughed out loud, but he quickly covered his mouth so no sound would come out. *Quiet, quiet, you must be quiet!*

Nevertheless, a small giggle escaped. Jasper pressed his face close to the window as Catherine Shelby picked up another gift. She passed it to her husband, who held it where Bess could see. She smiled feebly as her father showed her the gift. Mayor Shelby handed it to Andrew so he could unwrap it for Bess, who didn't appear to have enough energy.

It was a small porcelain horse, the purest white, with gold and blue designs painted delicately across it. Jasper thought it was the most beautiful thing he had ever seen. He'd spent every day for weeks in Mr. Finch's shop painting the figurines, but compared to the painting on this porcelain horse, his painting looked like it was done by a three-year-old. Bess smiled and reached out her hands for the horse. She admired the way it gleamed in the firelight, then clasped it close to her chest.

Jasper smiled.

More gifts were unwrapped, each one as lovely as the last. Jasper's heart felt full and happy. There was no day more wonderful than Christmas, no moment more precious than Christmas night. As he lay peering in at the window, palms pressed to the glass, watching those gifts being unwrapped, he wondered briefly why he always felt sad on Christmas. It was a happy time, wasn't it? Right now, in this moment, he could believe that next year would be better than this year had been. Something good would happen. There would be hope, and life, and change.

"Happy birthday, Jasper," he whispered to himself.

Jasper couldn't be sure, but for a brief moment, Bess's gaze seemed to wander up to the window that he was peering into. He froze in panic. *She can't see me, can she? What will she think? No, she definitely can't, it's too dark out here, too bright in there.*

If Bess did see him, though, she didn't do anything to give it away. Yet her left hand, Jasper noticed, lifted just slightly, almost imperceptibly. Was she waving at Jasper? He couldn't be sure, and soon, Mayor Shelby was lifting her to carry her to the supper table.

Jasper moved over to the dining room window and watched in rapture just like he did every year. All those delicious dishes! He imagined that *he* was the one tasting Mrs. Shelby's steaming pudding and lamb roast, soft and warm and rich with spice, and his mouth watered! Green beans and hot rolls and butter and mashed potatoes and yams and so many other dishes he couldn't count.

All too soon, it came to an end. Mrs. Shelby got Andrew to help her clear away the dishes. Mayor Shelby carried Bess up to her bedroom. George sat rolling peas across the table.

Until next year, Jasper thought. A sense of reverence came over him as he made his way to his favorite window. He dug down through the snow until he could see through it.

There was the nativity scene with Mary and Joseph and the three wisemen and all the rest. There was the beautiful crystal angel. It was time for his wish. Jasper licked his numb lips. Perhaps because of the snow storm or because Jasper was so enraptured in the Christmas celebrations, Jasper had all but forgotten what might happen if Henry Gersham stepped out onto his balcony and saw him there. But now, he was at the nativity window, in clear, plain sight of Henry Gerhsam's window, and a rush of fear washed over him.

Get on with it, Jasper, he thought to himself. *This is your chance! Make your wish and escape before he comes!*

But something in Jasper was curious to know. What was Christmas evening like for Henry Gersham?

He crawled away from the nativity window and trotted over to the Gershams' house. He dug his way down to the living room window and peered in.

It was another bright scene like the one through the Shelbys' window: Christmas tree, presents, shredded wrapping paper thrown around the room. But Jasper's eyes were drawn to the bed at one end of the room. There lay Henry Gersham, and he looked dreadful. The color had faded from his normally ruddy cheeks. His green eyes were bleary, and as Jasper watched, Henry coughed a nasty cough. He must have caught the fever from Bess, but he looked far worse. His mother held his hand

and forced a smile, but his father must not have been able to. He sat beside the fireplace and wept.

Jasper stared in the window until the cold got into his bones and he told himself it was time to leave. He made his way slowly back to the Shelbys' nativity window. He crouched in the snow, staring down at the crystal angel. For a long moment, all Jasper did was stare. Then he licked his numb lips and spoke quietly: "I wish . . . . I wish for Henry Gersham to get well."

Chapter 19

As the wish for Henry to get well spilled out of Jasper's mouth, he thought of his parents, and tears rushed to his eyes. He buried his face in his hands and wept. He was so alone and so cold, but mainly so alone. So terribly alone. Mr. Finch was leaving, Bess was ill, and he had no friends. *Perhaps,* he thought deep inside his heart, *it would have been better if I had never been born at all.*

Jasper couldn't stop his tears. They fell onto the crusty snow and rolled down toward the middle of the Shelbys' yard, where the top of Santa and his reindeer poked up from the deep drifts. The tears sunk into the snow until they touched Santa. And then, something very unusual happened.

The Santa, who had stood still decorating the yard of the Shelbys winter after winter, that Santa grunted and stirred, like an old man being woken from a nap.

Jasper didn't see this, of course, because his face was still buried in his hands as he cried. He cried and cried, his tears rolling down the snow to touch Santa's reindeer and the snow-man beside them. Suddenly, the reindeer tossed their heads, shaking the snow from their antlers. Their little bells on their harnesses jingled. The snowman yawned and stretched, then began to dig himself out of the snowdrift he was stuck in.

Santa Claus was already stomping his way out, straightening his coat and brushing snowflakes from his long white beard. He frowned when he saw Jasper crying beside the Shelbys' window. "What's this now?" Santa rumbled. "Tears? On Christmas?"

Jasper's head jerked up. His eyes went wide when he saw Santa, but he was too astonished to speak.

Santa put his hand on Jasper's shoulder and smiled a kindly smile. "This is a rare thing," he marveled. "A boy who would give his Christmas wish for someone else's good! And not just anyone else, but that naughty boy Henry, who does nothing but pick on you. Hmph!" Santa bent close to Jasper (who was still quite speechless), so close that his beard tickled Jasper's cheek. "I have merry tidings for you, Jasper," he said, his eyes all a-twinkle. "This year, your wish will come true."

"Henry—Henry will get well?" Jasper asked, finally finding his tongue.

Santa chuckled a great, rumbling chuckle. "No, no—though perhaps that wish will come true, too. But I am talking about the wish you've made all these years . . . ."

"To say *I love you* to my parents?" Jasper asked, wide-eyed.

Santa winked. "Just the one!"

Jasper looked around, all in a daze. "But where . . . . how . . . ?"

Santa put his hand once again on Jasper's shoulder. Jasper imagined it was much like how a grandfather would put his hand on his grandson's shoulder. "There are some wishes I can make true and some I cannot," he said solemnly. "I cannot bring your parents back to you, but I *can* give you the chance to tell them you love them. You'll find the answer to your wish back at the orphanage."

Without another thought, Jasper ran for the orphanage, slipping and scrambling over the snow. The Shelbys' front gate was buried in the snow, so he ran right over it and turned across the square, snow flying from his feet as he raced toward the road that led to McCallister's Orphanage. He heard a booming laugh behind him, and the jingling of silver bells.

"I'll spare you the journey!" Santa cried, and in a flash of red and gold, Jasper was swept off his feet. He cried out in surprise and delight as all of a sudden he was whisked above the tree-tops to glide through the starry sky in Santa's sleigh. The wind tossed his hair, and his stomach flipped with excitement as the sleigh sped up and flew higher.

Jasper's tears of loneliness turned to tears of joy. *I must be dreaming!* he thought. He whooped and hugged Santa. But the warm, velvety arms that hugged him back let him know that he wasn't dreaming. This was completely real.

"I don't want to go back to the orphanage! I don't want to ever go back! Can I stay with you? Can we ride in your sleigh every night?"

Santa laughed a jolly laugh. "There are things I cannot change, Jasper," he said fondly. "If you were to disappear from the orphanage, imagine how anxious Headmistress Cicely would be! She cares about you, you know."

Jasper nodded. He did know. He knew that she had to be stern to keep the children healthy and learning, and also that she had to spread what love she had across fifty boys, even more as they came and went, but it was there.

The cold night wind pressed tears from the corners of Jasper's eyes as Santa's reindeer pulled them through the sky. Jasper had never felt such joy in his life. He watched the reindeers' proud antlers reaching for the moon, all their bells a-jingle. Their hooves raced across the invisible heavens, their flanks steaming in the cold night air. They curved toward McCallister's Orphanage at a touch of Santa's reins. Down they went, drawing the sleigh after them. Jasper cried out in wonder. They sped past the treetops, and Jasper laughed as the sleigh dislodged a rain of snow from branches that it passed.

Jasper must have only flown for moments, but he felt suspended in time. The whole world was a white carpet beneath them with little toy houses and shops and streetlights. His toes tingled with joy. When Jasper looked down at them, he realized that, for the first time all month, they weren't searing with cold. The hole in his boot had magically smoothed over.

Santa winked. "You fix my boot, I fix yours."

Jasper laughed. "Hey," he said. "Can this sleigh do any tricks?"

Santa chuckled. "You're a brave one, aren't you? Well then, hold on tight."

Jasper gripped the sides of the sleigh and before he knew it, he was upside down and shouting with glee as they looped through the sky.

"That was amazing!" he cried as they straightened back out.

Santa gave a tug on the reins, then, and the sleigh began to slow. The jolly old man shouted out, "HO-HO-HO-hooome."

The orphanage drew into view, and for the first time in Jasper's life, it looked small and unthreatening, with firelight in its windows and smoke curling happily from its chimneys.

"I will get to tell my parents I love them here?" Jasper asked as Santa's sleigh touched down in front of the orphanage.

Santa gave him another wink. "Go inside straightaway and fall asleep in your bed," he advised.

Jasper climbed out of the sleigh, grinning. He waved Santa goodbye and patted each reindeer as he passed it. "Thanks for the ride!" He ran up the orphanage steps, through the door, down the hall, up the stairs, and into his room. All the other boys were already asleep. Jasper hurried to his bed. He threw off his coat and kicked off his boots. *Go inside straightaway and fall asleep in your bed*, Santa had said.

Jasper climbed into his bed and snuggled beneath the covers. His heart was racing, and Jasper didn't know how he would ever be able to make himself sleep. But then he told himself, *You're already dreaming, Jasper. Santa and the reindeer were all a dream to begin with.* He smiled sleepily. *A wonderful dream.*

Chapter 20

Jasper sank into sleep. It was a warm, comfortable sleep, unlike the cold sleeps he had so often, filled with shadows and bad dreams. In his sleep, he found himself walking in a green meadow. The sky above was blue, the trees around were green, and there were yellow butterflies flitting from flower to flower. Jasper turned in a circle, struck by the beauty of it all. "Mother?" he called. "Father?"

"Here we are, Jasper."

Jasper spun.

And there they were. He felt fire all up and down his spine. It held him where he was, barely daring to breathe. His mother walked closer, reaching for his hand. She smiled, and Jasper's heart nearly stopped. She was slender, beautiful, with auburn hair and smiling green eyes.

"Are you . . . . are you my mother?"

She knelt in front of him, taking her hands in her own. "Oh, my beautiful Jasper! Look how big you've grown." Reaching up, she took his head in her hands and kissed him on the brow.

Tears trickled down Jasper's cheeks. He threw his arms around his mother with a sob. Looking over her shoulder, he saw his father there. Dark-haired—*Like me*, Jasper thought—with strong arms and a smile that made Jasper feel like nothing would ever be frightening again. He reached past his mother, and his father took his hand. He kneeled beside Jasper's mother and wrapped his arms around Jasper.

"Jasper," his father whispered, tousling his hair. "You don't know how much I miss you."

Jasper buried his face in his father's shoulder and cried.

"We're so proud of you," his mother said in her loving voice. "So very proud of you, Jasper."

"You haven't had an easy life," his father said, "but you've grown into a good young man all the same. You've never lost your kind heart. That's all I could wish for in my son."

Jasper drew back from them and wiped the tears from his cheeks, a little embarrassed. His mother laughed and brushed away the next tear with her thumb. "I love you," Jasper mumbled. "I love you, I love you, I love you! I've waited years to tell you that."

His mother's eyes crinkled as she smiled. "Oh, Jasper. My son. You know what today is?"

"Christmas?" Jasper said.

"That, too," his father smiled.

His mother leaned close, the fragrance of her auburn hair swirling around Jasper. "It's your birthday, Jasper!" Her green eyes danced.

Jasper couldn't stop himself from smiling. "I'm nine," he said with a hint of proudness. It sounded so old, nearly ten.

"A young man," Jasper's father said. He took Jasper's shoulders in his hands and turned Jasper to face him. "Your mother and I have a birthday gift for you, son."

Jasper's breath caught. A birthday gift? No one had ever given him a birthday gift before! "May I . . . . may I see it?"

His mother held out a small, simple box. Jasper took it carefully. He stared down at it, heart racing.

"Open it," his mother urged with a smile.

Jasper took off the lid. Inside the box was a golden locket in the shape of a heart. Jasper lifted it delicately by its golden chain.

"Open it," his mother said again. She seemed impatient for him to see what was inside.

Jasper's fingers were trembling. He fumbled with the clasp for a second, then the locket flipped open. Inside, carved elegantly into the golden metal, was his name.

Jasper.

"I gave this locket to your mother when we were married," his father said, and all of a sudden, the meadow around Jasper whisked away. In its place he saw a scene from the past: his father, younger, giving a little parcel to his mother. It was wrapped in brown paper with white strings. When his mother opened it, she found the locket inside. A smile blossomed across her face. She threw her arms around his father's neck, and they twirled.

"I wore it all the time," Jasper heard his mother say. "Everywhere I went, I wore this locket."

The dream blurred together in front of Jasper's eyes, a hundred different scenes of his mother wearing the locket lovingly around her throat.

"When you were born," his father's voice came, "we inscribed your name on it, and your mother wore it close to her heart to think of you."

The scenes faded and the meadow returned, filled with the pleasant drone of bees buzzing from flower to flower. Jasper turned to his parents, who knelt in the grass in front of him. "You're giving this to me now?" he asked, holding the locket.

His mother smiled. "It belongs to you. So that you can remember us."

"And know how much we love you," his father said.

"Because we do love you, Jasper." His mother kissed him again on the forehead.

"With all our hearts," his father said, and he wrapped Jasper in his arms.

Jasper woke in his bed at the orphanage. He lay where he was, very still, for a long time. *What a wonderful dream,* he thought. *The best dream I've ever had.* Santa and the reindeer, flying through the night sky, meeting his parents and finally getting to tell them he loved them. He sighed and smiled. It had been the most splendid Christmas gift, that dream.

Jasper yawned, reaching under his pillow as he stretched. His fingers touched something metallic, and he stopped. He sat up and threw his pillow aside—and there it was, snuggled amid the wrinkles of his sheets.

The locket.

Jasper reached out, shaking, and picked it up. "It's real," he whispered. He opened it. There inside was his name, carved in loving letters. "It's *real!*" he cried again. "It was real!" He clutched the locket to his chest, laughing and sobbing at the same time. "I love you," he whispered, rocking back and forth with the locket pressed to his heart. "I love you! Oh, I wish I had gotten longer with you! You're so beautiful and wise, Mother, and Father you're so strong and kind."

Jasper shifted in his bed, and he heard the small, tinny sound of shillings brushing against one another. He reached under his mattress and pulled out the sock, nearly spilling over with the coins he had earned.

I wonder . . . .

Clutching the sock in his hand, Jasper leapt from the bed and thumped down the stairs without even bothering to put his shoes on. He flew down the shoveled tunnel from the or-phanage door in his pajamas.

"Mr. Finch!" he shouted. "Mr. Finch!" All the way into

town he ran, gripping the sock in white knuckles. "Mr. Finch!" Into the town square he raced, straight through a snowball fight, leaping over snow forts and dodging around snowmen. He skidded up to the carpenter's door and threw it open. The little bell jingled crazily.

"Mr. Finch!" Jasper ran up the stairs to the old man's bedroom above the shop. He burst through the door. "Will this be enough?" he demanded, shaking the sack of coins over the groggy carpenter.

Mr. Finch stirred from his bed. "What? Jasper? Is that you?"

"Will these be enough for one month's rent?" Jasper gasped. "I know it's not much, but after that, I'll keep helping you paint, and you don't need to pay me a thing. Sales have gone up since I've started painting, you said so, and every shilling will go toward the rent. Please, tell me these will be enough!"

Mr. Finch sat up in bed. His wispy white hair stuck out in all directions. "You worked hard to earn those shillings, Jasper. You can't just give them all away to a tired old man like me."

"Who says?" Jasper panted. He shook the sock of coins with a triumphant grin. "I decide, don't I? They're *my* coins." It sounded so good to say that, to say that something was *his*.

Mr. Finch looked unconvinced. "I wouldn't want you to—"

"But *I* want to," Jasper interrupted, flushed. "There's nothing I would rather buy than for you to stay."

Mr. Finch looked at Jasper for a second, then his lip began to tremble. Jasper watched, startled, as the old man's eyes filled with tears. "Oh, Jasper," he sobbed, and he wrapped his stringy old arms around Jasper.

Jasper hugged Mr. Finch for a long time. Eventually he said, "You know, I've only ever been hugged in my dreams before."

The old carpenter squeezed Jasper tighter. "You should have told me that weeks ago," he chuckled. He pulled back and took Jasper by the shoulders. "I never wanted to leave, Jasper. This is my home. This is where I raised my family. But I thought there was no other way, with the rent going up, and...You don't have to do this, you know?"

"Please don't say anymore, Mr. Finch. I want you to stay. I wouldn't know what to do if you left."

Mr. Finch smiled in relief. "Thank you, Jasper. Thank you."

Jasper grinned.

Mr. Finch frowned suddenly. "What's this?" He pushed aside the fringe of Jasper's shirt to show a glimmer of golden chain.

Jasper pulled out the locket, which he had tucked under his shirt. "It's my birthday gift," he said proudly.

When Jasper stepped out of the carpenter's shop twenty minutes later, a light snow was falling. He looked down at his feet and shivered. Mr. Finch had lent him a pair of his old boots for the walk back to the orphanage, but they were too large, and the cold air slipped right down to play among Jasper's toes.

Never mind. He was happy.

Jasper walked across the square to the Shelbys' mansion. He stood in the street staring at it, looking from one merry window to the next, lingering on the Christmas tree that stood proudly in the front window. Santa stood in his usual pose, looking up at the Gershams' house. Jasper beamed at him.

A couple of ladies passed on the sidewalk behind him, bundled elegantly in furs and winter velvets. Jasper didn't turn, but he recognized the voice of Henry Gersham's mother, high with excitement.

"...can't explain it," she said. "Last night he was worsening, but this morning he's right as rain! I was worrying myself over having to take him to see the doctors in the city, about the bad roads and his health and all of that, but we won't have to do that now. He's back to his normal self, and…"

Mrs. Gersham's voice trailed out of earshot. Jasper stood in the snow and thought about Henry Gersham being back to his normal self.

"Thank you, Santa," he whispered. He touched the locket around his neck. "You really do make wishes come true."

At long last, Jasper's eyes strayed up to Bess' bedroom window. It was lit cheerily by firelight.

Jasper wondered if Bess thought about him anymore, or if he had faded from her mind since that day at the pond. He tucked his locket carefully back under his shirt, and smiled. "If you don't think of me anymore," he said quietly, "I'll be alright."

He turned and started toward the orphanage. "But if you do think of me still . . . . well, that would be better."

Please Leave a Review!

Reviews greatly improve the chances of success of any book and are a great way for you to support Jasper's Magical Christmas.

If you enjoyed reading Jasper please register at www.benjaminwardak.com for notifications on upcoming books.

Made in the USA
Middletown, DE
12 November 2021